"Luzzi's new memoir transforms unthinkable tragedy into literary gold. More than simply a memoir of mourning, *In a Dark Wood* testifies to the life-giving importance of literature and what it has to teach us."

—BookPage.com

"Luzzi's story is intensely personal, but holds universal appeal for anyone who has experienced love and loss. As he grasps blindly for routes out of his personal underworld, both he and the reader discover that only a change of mind and heart can open the way to love and fulfillment."

—*Booklist*

"Luzzi honestly grapples with profound questions about being a man and father in this very literary and very personal work."

—*Publishers Weekly*

"A forthright chronicle of emergence from darkness." —*Kirkus Reviews*

"Luzzi has written a memoir that is at once inspiring and fascinating. Beautifully written, with humor as well as depth, this book is a must for all serious readers."

—*Hudson Valley News*

"You say you've not read *The Divine Comedy*. It doesn't matter. Luzzi writes with the economy and flair of a novelist . . . [and] we travel deep inside the emotional process by which the poet [Dante] used his imagination to construct a narrative to deal with grief. . . . Luzzi makes it all personal when he twines his historical analysis . . . with his own dark emotional terrain."

—*Chronogram*

"Luzzi adopts Dante's journey as his own. He writes about the long, difficult path through the hell of grief in search of healing, [exploring] the power that Dante's poetry still holds for modern audiences."

—*The Thread*, MPR News

"The book soared when Luzzi used Dante's words to explain how grief made him feel."

—*Salon*

In a
Dark Wood

ALSO BY JOSEPH LUZZI

My Two Italies

A Cinema of Poetry: Aesthetics of the Italian Art Film

Romantic Europe and the Ghost of Italy

HARPER PERENNIAL

NEW YORK • LONDON • TORONTO • SYDNEY • NEW DELHI • AUCKLAND

In a
Dark Wood

A Memoir

Joseph Luzzi

HARPER ● PERENNIAL

A hardcover edition of this book was published in 2015 by Harper Wave, an imprint of HarperCollins Publishers.

HarperCollins books may be purchased for educational, business, or sales promotional use. For information, please e-mail the Special Markets Department at SPsales@harpercollins.com.

In a Dark Wood is a work of nonfiction. Some names and identifying details have been changed.

FIRST HARPER PERENNIAL EDITION PUBLISHED 2016.

The Library of Congress has catalogued the hardcover edition as follows:
Luzzi, Joseph.
  In a dark wood : what Dante taught me about grief, healing, and the mysteries of love / Joseph Luzzi. — First edition.
    pages cm
    ISBN 978-0-06-235751-9 (hardback) —ISBN 978-0-06-235752-6 (paperback)—ISBN 978-0-06-235753-3 (ebook) 1. Dante Alighieri, 1265–1321. Divina commedia. 2. Dante Alighieri, 1265–1321—Influence. 3. Books and reading—Psychological aspects. 4. Meaning (Philosophy) in literature. 5. Luzzi, Joseph. 6. Grief—Biography. I. Title.
  PQ4390.L89 2015
  851'.1—dc23
  [B]
                                        2015001132

ISBN 978-0-06-235752-6 (pbk.)

HB 08.11.2022

For Isabel

l'amor che move il sole e l'altre stelle

Every grief story is a love story.

Contents

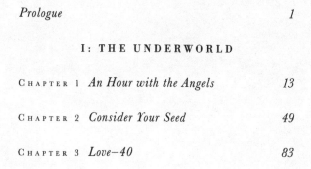

Prologue   *1*

I: THE UNDERWORLD

CHAPTER 1   *An Hour with the Angels*   *13*

CHAPTER 2   *Consider Your Seed*   *49*

CHAPTER 3   *Love–40*   *83*

II: MOUNT PURGATORY

CHAPTER 4   *Astrid and Anja*   *117*

CHAPTER 5   *The Gears of Justice*   *149*

CHAPTER 6   *Rough Draft*   *173*

Contents

III: ONE THOUSAND AND ONE

CHAPTER 7   *Posthoc7*   205

CHAPTER 8   *Fathers and Sons*   233

CHAPTER 9   *Open Hours*   257

Epilogue   283

Translations and Notes   291

Acknowledgments   295

In a
Dark Wood

Prologue

~~~

Nel mezzo del cammin di nostra vita, mi ritrovai per una selva oscura.

I n the middle of our life's journey, I found myself in a dark wood."

So begins one of the most celebrated and challenging poems ever written, Dante's *Divine Comedy*, a fourteen-thousand-line epic about the soul's journey through the afterlife. The tension between the pronouns says it all: although the "I" belongs to Dante, who died in 1321, his journey is also part of "our life." We will all find ourselves in a dark wood one day, the lines suggest.

For me that day came eight years ago, on November 29, 2007, a morning just like any other. I left my home in upstate New York at eight thirty a.m. and drove to nearby Bard College, where I am a professor of Italian. It was cold and wet, the air barely creased by the gray light. After my first class ended, I walked to my office to gather materials and then made my way to a ten thirty a.m. class.

I was joking with my students as we all settled in, when I noticed something unusual out of the corner of my eye: there was a security guard standing at the door.

"Look, they're coming to arrest me," I said, laughing. But the beefy security guard was not smiling.

"Are you Professor Luzzi?"

I've done nothing wrong, was my first thought.

"Yes—why?"

"Please come with me."

I edged outside the classroom and saw the associate dean and vice president of the college racing up the stairwell. I started running too, down the stairs and out of the building. There was a security van waiting for me.

Joe, your wife's had a terrible accident.

The words came from somewhere close, but they sounded muffled, as though passing through dimensions. Time and space were bending around me.

I was entering the dark wood.

EARLIER THAT MORNING AT NINE fifteen, my wife, Katherine Lynne Mester, pulled out of a gas station and into oncoming traffic, just a few miles from where I sat proctoring an exam in Italian. As close as she was, I didn't hear the crunching blow of the oncoming van into the soft aluminum pocket of her driver's side door, nor did I see the careening skid of her jeep as it swerved across the country highway and finally came to a full stop twenty feet from impact on the other side of the road. In the monastery-like silence of my classroom, I was unaware of the surging convoy of emergency response vehicles that were barreling up Route 9G, ready to rescue my wife from the tangle of metal and speed her to Poughkeepsie's Saint Francis Hospital a half hour away.

These emergency responders were not just carrying my wife: Katherine was eight and a half months pregnant with our first child. Soon after the security guard had appeared at my ten thirty class, a medical team performed an emergency cesarean on an unconscious Katherine, delivering our daughter Isabel, who was limp, pale, had no respiratory effort, and whose heart rate was inaudible. The doctors applied pressure ventilation by bag and mask—but one minute into her new life Isabel's heart rate was still slow and she had to be intubated. Slowly her heart rate rallied. Within ten minutes she was taking her first voluntary, spontaneous breaths.

Forty-five minutes after Isabel was born, Katherine died.

I had left the house at eight thirty; by noon, I was a widower and a father.

A WEEK LATER, I FOUND myself standing in the cold rain in a cemetery outside of Detroit, watching as my wife's body was returned to the earth close to where she was born. The words for the emotions I had known until then—pain, sadness, suffering—no longer made sense, as a feeling of cosmic, paralyzing sorrow washed over me. My personal loss felt almost beside the point: a young woman who had been vibrant with life was now no more. I could feel part of me going down with Katherine's coffin. It was the last communion I would ever have with her, and I have never felt so unbearably connected to the rhythms of the universe. But I was on forbidden ground. Like all other mortals, I would have to return to the planet earth of grief. An hour with the angels is about all we can take.

Days afterward, I went for a walk in the village where Katherine and I had been living, Tivoli, New York. By chance I ran into a neighbor who was also out walking: the chaplain who had officiated at my college's memorial service for Katherine.

"You're in hell," she said to me.

I immediately thought of Dante, the author I had devoted much of my career to teaching and writing about. After a charmed youth as a leading poet and politician in Florence, Italy, the city where he was born in 1265, Dante Alighieri was sentenced to exile while on a diplomatic mission. In those first years, Dante wandered around the region of Tuscany, desperately seeking to return to his beloved city. He met with fellow exiles, plotted military action, connived with former enemies—anything to get home. But he never set foot in Florence again. His words on the experience would become a mantra to me:

You will leave behind everything you love
most dearly, and this is the arrow
the bow of exile first lets fly.

No other words could capture how I felt during the four years I struggled to find my way out of the dark wood of grief and mourning. And yet it was only because of his exile that Dante was able to write *The Divine Comedy*, when he accepted once and for all that he would never return to Florence. Before 1302, the year he was expelled, he had been a fine lyric poet and an impressive scholar. But he had yet to find his voice. Only in exile did he gain the heaven's-eye view of human life, detached from all earthly allegiances, that enabled him to speak of the soul.

At the beginning of *The Divine Comedy*, as Dante finds himself lost in the *selva oscura*—the dark wood—he sees a shade in the distance. It's his favorite writer, the Roman poet Virgil, author of *The Aeneid* and a pagan adrift in the Christian afterworld. By way of greeting, Dante tells Virgil that it was his *lungo studio e grande amore*—his long study and great love—that led him to the ancient poet. Virgil becomes Dante's teacher on ethics, willpower, and the cyclical nature of human mortality, illustrated by his metaphor of the souls in hell bunched up like fallen leaves. Virgil is his guide through the dark wood, just as *The Aeneid* gave Dante the tools he needed to curb his grief over losing Florence, whose splendor would haunt him as he wandered through Italy looking for a home during the last twenty years of his life.

That's beauty's terrible calculus, I would come to learn: its hold over you becomes stronger after you've lost it.

I had met Katherine four years earlier at an art opening in Brooklyn, her tall, elegant beauty standing out amid the slouching hipsters in T-shirts and flannel. She was wearing a form-fitting dress and stood with perfectly erect posture as she drank her champagne and talked with a friend. I made a bee-line for her and mustered up the courage to introduce myself. She was kind enough not to sneer at my opening line.

"Nice shoes," I said, pointing to her spectacular leopard print heels.

"They are, aren't they?" she answered smiling.

And with these few words my life began to flow in a new direction, one of brief but powerful happiness, the kind that changes you. The crowd buzzing around us seemed to disappear as Katherine told me about her family in suburban Detroit, the father she adored who was a federal judge and a pillar of their community. She laughed as she described her mother, a homemaker who had been raised on a cherry farm and now rankled the family with her unfiltered outbursts on subjects ranging from America's welfare system to children who pursue artistic careers. I learned about Katherine's fancy prep school that the family could hardly afford and that she could barely stay afloat in, and her years of fruitless auditions and demos: "My mom says stop doing freebies," she joked. We walked through the warm October night, first in a pack, then just the two of us. I told her I was a professor, and she repeated the word slowly, looking me in the eye. I don't know whether she was impressed or just glad to meet somebody from a staid world far from her own. By two in the morning, we were in a cab that would drop me off in Park Slope and then take her to the Upper West Side. But there was a terrible thud, and the car stopped stock-still in the middle of a Brooklyn thoroughfare.

"Sorry, man," the driver shouted back to us, "we've got a flat."

Katherine and I had fallen asleep next to each other, but now were jolted awake by the noise. Earlier in the evening, I had punched her number into my cell phone, and as we waited for the driver to fix the tire, I couldn't help but worry that my phone could also experience a mechanical failure, just like the cab.

Later, alone in my apartment, my concern turned to panic: what if I had taken her number down incorrectly? I had no other way of contacting her, no last name, address, or mutual friends. In my southern Italian superstition, I wondered if the jolt from the flat tire was an ominous sign—that I might have lost our connection for good.

Forty-eight hours later, I dialed the number and she picked up on the first ring.

NOTHING KATHERINE AND I SHARED could prepare me for the challenges that would come when our allotted time was over. Rilke once wrote that to love another person is our ultimate task, that for which all else is preparation. Only after losing this love did I grasp his awful wisdom. One of you will have to face the world alone someday and inhabit the Underworld—the hell at the start of Dante's descent into a dark wood.

A car accident claimed Katherine's body, but my grief would nearly kill her memory. For the longest time after her death, she became opaque, as an unconscious force deep inside me repressed the things that we had shared. I didn't try to distance myself from my most intense recollections of her, from the feel of her skin against my own or her smell in the morning as sleep still clung to her. Before I met Katherine I used to believe that love's chosen space was night, the time for coupling in the dark and dreaming in tandem. But Katherine heightened the start of each day, from the first light that fell on her through the blinds beside the bed, illuminating the dust in chiaroscuro stripes, to the rhythmic weight of her breath, as heavy on my shoulders as her resting arms. Surrounded by her sleeping body, I felt love's gravity, and it took all of my strength to disentangle myself from her and follow the streams of brightly lit dust out of the bed and into the new day. Slowly but implacably, her death began to transform these living sensations into spectral images—things that haunted my dreams and daydreams, but which I could no longer feel or smell or taste. Grief was a great disembodier.

The insulating shock that kept me from absorbing the full pain of Katherine's loss also numbed me, preventing me from recalling the full joy of what we had shared. The love we had made, the promises we had exchanged, the plans we had scribbled on Sunday afternoon scraps of paper—grief carried them all away. Only years later, when I began to write about this lost cache of memory, would I learn that to survive Katherine's loss I had to let her die a second time, in my thoughts and dreams, so that the pain would not paralyze me.

The day of her accident, part of my shock was tempered by the calming thought that I could speak with her later that night in spirit—after all, our relationship had been cut short almost mid-conversation. But these one-way dialogues offered only the coldest comfort; I needed a guide, someone who knew how to speak with the dead. Someone who had written about life in the dark wood.

The Divine Comedy didn't rescue me after Katherine's death. That fell to the support of family and friends, to my passion for teaching and writing, and above all to the gift of my daughter. Our daughter. But I would barely have made my way without Dante. In a time of soul-crunching loneliness—I was surrounded everywhere by love, but such is grief—his words helped me withstand the pain of loss.

After years of studying Dante, I finally heard his voice. At the beginning of *Paradiso* 25, he bares his soul:

Should it ever happen that this sacred poem,
to which both heaven and earth have set hand,
so that it has made me lean for many years,
should overcome the cruelty that bars me
from the fair sheepfold where I slept as a lamb,
an enemy to the wolves at war with it . . .

I still lived and worked and socialized in the same places and with the same people after my wife's death. And yet I felt that her death exiled me from what had been my life. Dante's words gave me the language to understand my own profound sense of displacement. More important, they enabled me to connect my anguished state to a work of transcendent beauty.

After Katherine died, I obsessed for the first time over whether we have a soul, a part of us that outlives our body. The miracle of *The Divine Comedy* is not that it answers this question, but that it inspires us to explore it, with *lungo studio e grande amore*, long study and great love.

This journey began for me thirty years ago in a ferocious part of Italy.

I

The Underworld

. . . BOYS AND UNWED GIRLS
AND SONS LAID ON THE PYRE BEFORE THEIR PARENTS' EYES.

CHAPTER 1

An Hour with the Angels

La bocca sollevò dal fiero pasto.

He lifted up his mouth from the savage meal.

My uncle Giorgio recited this line to me when I was a college student visiting Italy for the first time, on my junior year abroad in Florence in 1987. A shepherd and rail worker who had never spent a day in school, Giorgio spoke neither English nor standard Italian—yet he spoke Dante. We were sitting around the table in his tiny kitchen, my ears buzzing with the dialect phrases of my childhood. Giorgio decanted glasses of his homemade wine as he welcomed me to Calabria, the region on the toe of the Italian peninsula whose *la miseria*—an untranslatable term meaning relentless hardship—my parents had escaped thirty years earlier when they immigrated to America.

For three days, I followed Giorgio and his son Giuseppe from one village to the next. Everyone we met—women in sackcloth, men with missing teeth—welcomed me as though I were a foreign dignitary. I never asked Giorgio how he had managed to learn some Dante by heart, and I doubt that he knew any of the actual plot of *The Divine Comedy*. It didn't matter: he knew its music. Here, in the south of Italy, as far from the Renaissance splendor of Florence as you could get, he was a living and breathing trace of Dante's presence.

Giorgio's words stayed with me on the long train ride back to Florence, bringing me inside one of the most chilling scenes in *The Divine Comedy*: the one in which the traitor Ugolino lifts up his head from the man he has been condemned to cannibalize for eternity, Archbishop Ruggieri, to tell Dante how he ended up devouring his own children in the prison tower where Ruggieri had locked them. I was reading Dante for the first time, in a black Signet paperback translation by John Ciardi, while also trying to get through the original Tuscan. But nothing brought him to life like my uncle's declaration.

Back in Florence, Dante was everywhere. Outside the Basilica of Santa Croce, a few blocks from my school, a nineteen-foot-high statue of the poet looked down sternly on the square, as though guarding the church where Machiavelli, Michelangelo, Galileo, and the nation's founding fathers are buried.

A few blocks north, the neighborhood where Dante grew up spread toward Brunelleschi's Duomo. I had never taken a class on *The Divine Comedy* before my trip to Florence, but my visit to Calabria had shown me that its verses could live outside of libraries and museums and inside the huts and fields of my parents' homeland. Dante's simple, sober Tuscan-Italian made me feel the ground beneath me. I could smell his language.

S'ïo avessi le rime aspre e chiocce, / come si converrebbe al tristo buco . . .

"If I had verses harsh and grating enough / to describe this wretched hole," Dante writes at the beginning of *Inferno* 32 to describe the depths of hell. He was as gritty and local as the Calabrian world my parents had abandoned. I plowed through the Ciardi and muddled through the Tuscan. For the first time in my life, I was inhabiting a book.

The capaciousness of *The Divine Comedy*—with its high poetry, dirty jokes, literary allusions, farting noises—floored me. I marveled at Dante's universe of good and evil, love and hate, all ordered by unfaltering eleven-syllable lines in rhyming tercets. He communicated vast amounts of knowledge, medieval and ancient, without drowning out the music of his verse. He knew his Bible and his classics cold. He distilled the latest gossip about promiscuous poets, gluttonous pals, and treacherous politicians. He knew which acclaimed thirteenth-century humanist had been accused of sodomy, and he dared write about the birth of the soul and the prestige of his own Tuscan. In *The Divine Comedy*, I had discovered my guide, from the high culture of the Florentine cobblestones to the earthy customs of the Calabrian shepherds.

The Divine Comedy, I had come to learn, was a book of many firsts: one of the the first epic poems written in a local European language instead of Latin or Greek; the first work to speak about the Christian afterlife while paying an equal amount of attention to our life on earth; the first to elevate a woman, Beatrice, into a full-fledged guide to heaven. But these weren't the innovations that most enthralled me—it was Dante's groundbreaking ability to speak intimately with his readers. His twenty addresses leapt off the page and into my daydream: "O you who have sound reasoning, / consider the meaning that is hidden / beneath the veil of these strange verses," he writes in *Inferno* 9. I could feel him speaking to me directly as I sat in my apartment in Piazza della Libertà, his rasping consonants and singing vowels drowning out the roar of the Vespas and the rumble of the traffic converging on the city's nearby ring roads. I felt I could spend a lifetime exploring the mystery of his *versi stani*, strange verses.

Soon after my visit to Calabria, Dante's words and his image had become, as he writes at the opening of *Paradiso*, a blessed kingdom stamped on my mind. I pictured him in Botticelli's famous portrait: in regal profile, with his magnificent aquiline nose launched ahead of his piercing stare, his body swathed in a crimson cloak, and his head crowned with a black laurel, the symbol of poetic excellence given an otherworldly gravitas by the brooding color. It was a face that had been to hell and back, visited the dead and lived to tell. And it was a burning gaze that would buckle under none of life's mysteries.

One late night in Florence I was out walking when I was arrested by a smell. I followed the scent and landed inside one of the city's *pasticcerie*, pastry shops, making the next morning's delicacies. I ordered a few brioches and took them to Santa Croce. In an empty square, I put the warm, achingly delicious pastry into my mouth as I leaned against the base of Dante's statue. I was in Italy, I thought—not my parents' Italy but another one, hundreds of miles from Zio Giorgio's Calabria and light years from the mud and sorrow that my family had left behind. Dante had somehow appeared in both places.

With my mouth filled with flakes of buttery pastry, I pressed my back against Dante and stared onto the silent stones of Santa Croce.

I was falling in love.

THE DAY AFTER KATHERINE DIED, I returned to our home after spending the night in the hospital. Her morning coffee was still out by the bathroom sink, where strands of her hair lay in coils. The bed was unmade and the drawers flung open, suggesting a day open to all sorts of possibilities. She had left the apartment to attend class at a local university, where she was completing her degree after giving up on acting. We had plans to meet for dinner, and she had used my favorite coffee cup, the Deruta ceramic mug with the dragon design that I had paid too much for in Florence.

I took the sheets in my arms and breathed in her smell one last time.

My family, who had come from Rhode Island the moment they heard the news, surrounded me. Choking back sobs, my mother and sisters put on latex gloves and set out to erase Katherine's last traces with Lysol and Formula 409.

The snow was falling outside—the first storm of the year.

Meanwhile, Isabel slept in a sterile forest of incubators in the neonatal unit of Poughkeepsie's Vassar Brothers Hospital, its machines nourishing her after an improbable birth. They would keep her safe while I went out walking, looking for souls bunched up like fallen leaves on the shores of the dead.

The snow fell nonstop after Katherine's accident, covering our village and announcing an early winter. The chaplain had told me I was in hell, but in my many walks around a dim, gloomy Tivoli, I felt more like I was in Virgil's Underworld—a place of shadows, no brimstone and fire. I thought of Dante losing his *"bello ovile,"* "fair sheepfold." During his lifetime, two political parties, the Guelphs and the Ghibellines, dominated Florentine politics and were perpetually at war with each other. Dante was a Guelph, which was usually pro-papacy. But in the intensely factional and family-based world of Florentine politics, a split in Dante's party emerged, and he joined the group that resisted Pope Boniface VIII's meddling in the city's affairs. This infuriated Boniface, who arranged to have Dante detained while he was in Rome on a diplomatic mission in 1302. Meanwhile, back in Florence, Dante's White Guelph party lost control of the city to the pro-papacy Black Guelphs, who falsely accused Dante of selling political favors and sentenced him to exile in absentia, ordering him to pay an exorbitant fine. Dante insisted that he was innocent and refused to pay. The Black Guelphs responded with an edict condemning Dante to permanent exile. *If you come back to Florence,* they warned, *you will be burned alive.* As I walked through the winterscape pondering Dante's fate, fire was the last element on my mind. But I could feel the edict's heat burn inside as the reality of my own exile descended upon me with each snowflake.

Dante would spend the first thirty-four cantos of *The Divine Comedy* at the degree zero of humanity, Inferno. His guide Virgil had also sung of hell in *The Aeneid,* of the Trojan hero Aeneas who watched Troy, sacked by the Greeks, burn to the ground, and then abandoned his lover Dido, Queen of Carthage, because the gods had decreed that he must forsake all entanglements to found Rome. At the book's end, Aeneas confronts his defenseless enemy Turnus, who had killed his friend Pallas. "Go no further down the road of hatred," Turnus begs him, and for a moment Aeneas relaxes the grip on his sword. But then he drives his sword into Turnus's breast, burying the hilt in his throat—*ira terribilis.* Terrible in his rage.

My own grief wasn't so ferocious. I could feel myself retreating into a cocoon, just like the one my mother made each night when she went to sleep, even in the dead of summer: the door shut, the windows sealed, the blankets pulled over her head. I wondered how she managed not to suffocate. Now I too needed total darkness. I started sleeping in the fetal position like my infant daughter.

One night I dreamed that I was back in the hospital the day of Katherine's accident, and someone was telling me that she was alive. In critical condition, but alive. I ran out of the room and shouted to my mother and four sisters, *"Is it true? Is she okay?"* The adrenaline surged through me, my heart nearly exploding out of my chest.

I woke up coated in sweat, a pool of vomit welling in my stomach. It had only been a dream, not a premonition.

I became so frightened of these visions that I tried to prepare for them. *Katherine is gone, Katherine is gone,* I repeated to myself each night before I went to sleep, just as I had on the day she died, when I slept in a hospital room adjacent to the incubating Isabel, my mother and sister beside me. Yet the reel would not stop. One dream had Katherine and me in a car, her flesh creamy to the touch, a life-breathing pink. I asked her why she had gone, how she could do such a thing, but she just sat there in impenetrable, lunar silence. In another dream we were in a crisis, on the brink of a breakup, a situation we had never remotely approached.

I know what you're doing, I'm saying to her, *you're trying to split up with me, for my own good, but I just can't do it. I'm not ready. Please don't leave me . . .*

I'm begging her, just as I had begged the neurosurgeon to save her when he and his team operated on Katherine's pummeled brain after Isabel was born.

Please, I said to him, *do anything. Hook her up to a machine, I don't care, just keep her alive!*

I sat waiting in a small room in Poughkeepsie's Saint Francis Hospital while they operated. A social worker was there beside me, along with a gray unsmiling nun who muttered something about the power of prayer. I left the room and found the hospital chapel, where I got down on my knees on a yellow polyurethane pew. A jaundiced-looking Jesus hung on a suspended cross.

Please, God. I beg you. Just keep her alive . . .

Then I made the fatal mistake of allowing myself a daydream.

"You gave us quite a scare," I'm saying, while I hold Katherine's hand and stroke her bruised body. But she doesn't answer. As in the dreams that would follow, she can no longer speak.

I left the chapel. The neurosurgeon appeared in tears.

ALL YE WHO ENTER ABANDON HOPE—Dante inscribed these words on the gates of hell. But after Katherine died it wasn't the lack of hope that was crushing me. It was the memory of what I had lost.

In 2004, Katherine and I began living together in North Carolina, where I had received a one-year fellowship at the National Humanities Center, enabling me to take a leave of absence from my regular teaching duties at Bard and focus on my scholarly research. Katherine had finally said good-bye to acting and given up her life in New York to join me in the South, as I gave up my apartment in Brooklyn with plans to move to the Bard area with Katherine after the fellowship ended. I arrived in North Carolina a few weeks before she did and set up our home while she completed a Pilates training course in New York. On the day she joined me, we went for a walk on Duke's East Campus, the struggles of living in New York with too little money dissolving in the warm air as we walked past the colonial facades and scattered gazebos. I thought, *If only we could stay here forever*, extend my one-year fellowship into an eternity. I had recently turned thirty-seven, nearly the same age as Dante when he found himself in the dark wood. Unlike Dante, however, I had little to show for myself—no family of my own, no relationship where I had given of myself completely, until I met Katherine.

Soon after we arrived, I came home on a warm fall afternoon to watch game three of the Red Sox's divisional playoff against the Yankees. My team was sure to lose, I told myself as I left my car and walked toward our warehouse loft in one of Durham's former tobacco factories, but I still savored the anticipation of the game. I grew up loving the Boston Red Sox, an experience that taught me we can't bend the world to our will, that life is in large part learning how to manage disappointment. In 1978, as a sixth grader on my way home from school, I listened as the neighborhood rang with the news: *Yaz just homered!* The Red Sox took a brief lead in their one-game playoff against the Yankees, only to fritter it away on an improbable home run by the beefcake Bucky Dent in the seventh. The great Carl Yastrzemski himself would seal the inevitable disaster, popping up on the blur of a Goose Gossage fastball that I knew was unhittable even before it skimmed harmlessly off his bat. It would take another twenty-six years for the curse of the Red Sox to lift.

Sitting in our North Carolina home, I watched helplessly as, by the ninth inning and down 4–3, it looked as though fate would hand the star-crossed Red Sox another loss. But then, after a startling rally against the otherwise invincible Mariano Rivera, the Red Sox's Big Papi Ortiz ended it all in extra innings with a mammoth game-winning home run. The Red Sox went on to win game four of seven as part of their improbable run to their first World Series title in nearly a hundred years.

Three years later, in fall 2007, Katherine and I were husband and wife and awaiting our first child, and the Red Sox were back in the playoffs. As I watched Game Six of their American League Championship against the Cleveland Indians, Katherine spoke on the phone with her mom. Our spacious apartment looked out onto Tivoli's main street and was perched above a gallery. There was an art opening that evening, so our floor hummed with voices and the shuffling of feet. The streets were filled with people walking to bars and restaurants. With the count three balls and a strike, the Red Sox's J. D. Drew was offered a fastball down the middle of the plate. With a graceful swing, he sent the ball sailing over the center field wall to give the Red Sox an insurmountable lead.

After Drew's hit, I walked out onto our porch and stood against the railing with a glass of wine in my hand. It was a pleasant November night, the air moist. The scraping of chairs and scuffling of feet in the gallery below had ceased, as the artists and guests spilled onto the sidewalk below me. Across the street, a vegetarian restaurant and country hotel gave off a warm glow through their frosted windows. The world felt small and ordered. I lived in a two-room loft that stood a short drive from the garden-like campus where I taught great books and a beautiful language, and inside our well-lit home my wife held our future in the perfect dome of her expanding belly. All I needed and wanted was right here in the life my wife and I had built amid the stacks of books and stray tennis rackets. While Katherine talked and J. D. Drew circled, I thought: *I have it all.* Not in the grand sense—no fame, fortune, or power. But in a good, simple way that was all I could hope for. For the first time, I could feel the sawed-off halves of my life—the family-oriented immigrant warmth I had grown up with and the striving, exciting, but exhausting climb up the academic mountain—coalescing into a whole. *The great is the enemy of the good,* according to an old Italian proverb, warning us away from chasing an unreachable ideal. Finally, at the age of forty, I was ready to accept the good.

This was October 2007, and the Red Sox eventually took the game and went on to win another World Series—their second in three years.

IN DECEMBER OF 2007, JUST two months after J. D. Drew sent the Red Sox into the World Series, I returned to the same spot where I had sipped my wine and contemplated my happiness. Then it had been a warm and moist early fall night; now snow covered the main street. Isabel slept in my bedroom and my mother was watching *Two and a Half Men* in the living room. The white desert outside my window brought to mind the words of Dante's greatest lover: "There is no greater pain / than to remember happy times / in misery." I was awake, but there was little difference between my daydreams and the dreams I had at night. Everything I imagined was a picture from the past that carried ominous implications for the future. It was like prophecy in reverse, with my greatest sorrow hidden in the folds of what had been my happiest thoughts—in a mind now held in fixed orbit by death.

"Tu pur morrai." You will die.

That's what the ladies with the crazy hair said to Dante in his first book, *La Vita Nuova* (*The New Life*), an autobiography that he wrote when he was in his twenties (about 1293)—a book about daydreams too terrible for words and the overpowering enigma of first love. A mixture of poetry and prose, the *Vita Nuova* narrates how Dante came to discover poetry as his life's calling, and how his love for writing was fueled by his passion for a young Florentine woman named Beatrice Portinari, who also went by her nickname, Bice. Both Dante and Beatrice belonged to Florence's nobility—but Beatrice's family stood on a higher ledge than Dante's, making him jealous.

On May 1, 1274, Beatrice's father, the wealthy banker Folco Portinari, invited the nine-year-old Dante and his family to a party celebrating the coming of spring. All it took was one look at Beatrice, Dante writes in the *Vita Nuova*, for him to fall head-long and hopelessly in love. The feeling wracked his body like a deadly airborne virus, nearly killing him:

> At that very moment, and I speak the truth, the vital spirit, the one that dwells in the most secret chamber of the heart, began to tremble so violently that even the most minute veins of my body were strangely affected; and trembling, it spoke these words: *Ecce deus fortior me, qui veniens dominabitur michi.*

"Here is a god stronger than I who comes to rule over me." With these Latin words—the ancient language meant to convey the authority of his new master, Love—Dante proclaims Beatrice's dominion over his heart. He would not see her again for another nine years, when he was eighteen and she seventeen. When he finally does, the illness returns, reducing him to uncontrollable tears and forcing him into the shameful privacy of his bedroom.

The *Vita Nuova* describes how these visions of Beatrice continue to inspire a mix of ecstasy and anguish in Dante. One day he falls ill, very ill, afflicted by a painful disease that makes him languish in bed for nine days. On the ninth day, he has a vision that is even more terrifying than his illness: the wild-haired ladies appear in his delirium, announcing, *"Tu pur morrai."*

One even tells him that he is already dead. Another says to him that Beatrice, his miraculous lady, has departed from this world.

The delirium breaks. He realizes it was all a dream: Beatrice still lives. But not for long. The vision was actually
a premonition. They may have been wearing sumptuous
robes, Dante realizes, but the women with the disheveled
hair were witches.

Terrified of my own daydreams and desperate for help, I
left the chilled balcony and phoned the chaplain whom I had
encountered my first snowy day in the Underworld.

A FEW DAYS AFTER I called the chaplain, she and I met at a
coffee shop near campus in the village of Red Hook.

An ordained minister, Georgia was a curly-haired
woman in her fifties, with gentle eyes and small shoulders
that sat incongruously on a large lower frame. She lived
just up the road from my apartment. I often saw her out
walking and would occasionally run into her at the Tivoli
library. During the memorial service for Katherine at Bard
she had been a calm, dignified presence, and when I saw
her walking in the snow I felt as though she had been sent
to help me.

I told her that I had been trying to connect with God. I
had been reading the Bible, annotating the margins of the
edition I had been given for my Catholic confirmation. I
tried to identify with Job, but he was too old, his suffering impossibly extravagant. I tried to pray, I told Georgia,
even got down on my knees on the hardwood floor of my
apartment, just as I was taught to do as a child—just as I

had in the yellow chapel of St. Francis Hospital in Poughkeepsie as the neurosurgeons worked on Katherine's trau-
matized brain. Dante believed that prayer expedited your
way through Purgatory to Paradise, with hundreds of years
lopped off in a single fervent supplication. Countless letters
were arriving, from my friends, Katherine's friends, our
families, my colleagues, people I grew up with, long-lost
connections. I even received consoling words from Leila
Cooper, a playmate from my childhood and the first girl
I ever had a crush on. The mother of one of my students,
a woman I had never met, wrote to say that I was in her
prayers. During the funeral in Detroit, hundreds of my
father-in-law's friends told me that they were praying for
me. I would instinctively answer: *pray for Isabel*. But my own
praying felt too staged to be genuine.

I confessed my guilt to Georgia. I knew it was irrational, but
I somehow felt responsible for my wife's death. I regretted that I
wasn't with her that morning. And, although I had tried to take
good care of Katherine, I could not shake the feeling that I had
failed to protect her.

"A better man would not have pushed Katherine so hard
to succeed in school, to bring in extra money, right?" I
asked.

"You're a victim, not a culprit," she answered.

She said that when someone God loves dies, he too feels unbearable sorrow. *He watched His own son die,* she said, sensing
that I was neither a natural believer nor a committed atheist.

She saw me for what I was: someone who hates confrontation and seeks the middle way, a person who had never professed his faith explicitly and categorically. I had always treated religion like a buffet—a little prayer here, a bit of compassion there, a sampling of cosmic love to top off the meal. But I knew that real faith meant choices, which required admitting what you did not believe in as much as what you did believe. In a realm calling for decisive feeling, I was hedging my spiritual bets. I was a diplomat even with faith.

Only the terror of my wife's death could bring me to my knees in prayer. But that didn't bother Georgia. She knew I needed to hear the words of a believer. By the end of our coffee, she was telling me about her favorite Italian films. We made plans to meet again soon.

But that would be our last conversation. I had revealed my darkest thoughts because she was a stranger, but this also stopped me from telling her more. For that, I would have to find someone I shared a history with, someone familiar. Like the man I had leaned against in Piazza Santa Croce. Ever since that night in Florence, I had turned to Dante with demanding questions, none more so than the ones I was now facing. Could I love Katherine now that her body was gone? I wondered. The question reminded me of a phrase that haunted me: *There is no love that is not physical.* I had encountered the words in a reading long ago whose source I no longer remembered, and its mysterious wisdom had remained lodged in my brain. Dante did not write it, but his poetry led me back to those words. For he had done the unthinkable: he made his most erotic lover a woman without a body.

THE VISIONS OF LOVE THAT terrified Dante in the *Vita Nuova* returned when he began his masterpiece, *The Divine Comedy*, about ten years later. Unlike most artists and writers in his Christian world, Dante understood that the sinners in hell and the saints in heaven burn with an equal amount of love. The difference between these two groups was not in the intensity of love's flames but in what kindled them. And in hell, passion's fire found an especially dry, combustible source in the heart of Francesca da Rimini.

Before Dante's imagination got hold of her, Francesca had been mentioned only once in a written source: a line in her father's will. Dante crafted her story out of legend, hearsay, and gossip. He didn't exactly make her up—but his poetry immortalized her. He did so around 1305, when he started to write *The Divine Comedy* after a few years wandering around Tuscany, trying to get back to Florence—living in the past and incapable of imagining a life outside of Florence. Once he finally accepted that he was never going to make it back, he embraced his own exile and the new perspective it offered. He reignited his imagination with a poetic fire that blazed with Francesca's love for Paolo.

Francesca was born in 1255, ten years before Dante. She was the daughter of Guido da Polenta, the ruler of Ravenna, a small city on the Adriatic with close ties to the Byzantine

Empire. As the daughter of her city's first family, she enjoyed all the status and wealth a young woman could hope for. But as a thinking and feeling creature, Francesca endured nothing but obstacles. Her patriarchal society didn't allow her to apply her talents to a career or calling. Worst of all, in matters of the heart she had to follow orders, not her heart.

The courtly love ethos of her time separated love from marriage: since most unions among the wealthy classes were based on dowries and social standing, the marital bed was the last place to look for passion. To love someone, it was understood by the educated classes, meant to worship from afar and to suffer. You could never possess your lover. But as you surrendered to the magnetic attractions of the one you loved—those virtues that actual sexual contact would only sully—your heartbroken spirit soared with the angels.

Francesca's father, Guido, brokered a marriage between her and Giovanni Malatesta, scion of a rival family. In uniting his daughter with the enemy, the pragmatic Guido aimed to bring peace to his people. His plan worked—as long as Francesca paid the price. Giovanni and Francesca were a grinding mismatch. She was beautiful; his nickname was Gianciotto, John the Lame, a reference to his disfigured body. Worse still, Francesca was a dreamer, easily enraptured by romantic sentiments and melodious turns of phrase. The soldierly Gianciotto would have scorned such reverie.

Francesca came of age during a poetic movement called the *Dolce Stil Novo* (Sweet New Style). For these poets, love wasn't an emotional state. It was an illness that crippled the body and clouded the mind. *Sospiri*, sighs. *Sbigottito*, bewildered. *Dolente*, suffering. *Paura*, fear. Francesca encountered these Sweet New Style words each time she turned the page and read of love. This language of desire filled her thoughts that fateful day in 1275 when she, a bride of twenty, first set eyes on Paolo—Gianciotto's handsome younger brother.

One of Dante's most astute readers, the Argentine writer Jorge Luis Borges, said that it takes a modern novel hundreds of pages to lay bare a character's soul, but Dante needs only a few lines. Borges must have been thinking of Francesca. No character enters *The Divine Comedy* as magnificently. In *Inferno* 5, Dante sees a couple in the distance who seem to float on the air, impervious to the gale-force winds that punish the lustful. Dante begs Virgil to speak to these windswept lovers, who approach him like doves. The woman speaks, thanking Dante for his invitation, calling him an *animal grazïoso*. Literally: gracious animal. What could be more flattering?

She tells Dante she was born on the shores of the Po River, and asks him the line that would come to haunt me: is there anything more horrible than remembering happy times in times of misery? Meanwhile, her beautiful partner Paolo stands beside her in total silence, streaming tears. Francesca even recites a poem for Dante: *Amor, ch'al cor gentil ratto s'apprende.* Love, which is quick to claim the gentle heart. As we listen to her speak, we begin to understand that Francesca's "love" isn't such a lofty emotion after all. It's a bona fide Sweet

New Style sickness. She describes how one day she and Paolo were reading King Arthur's tales, and they came across the passage where Arthur's wife, Guinevere, gives the knight Lancelot a fateful, adulterous kiss. The scene inspires her and Paolo to do the same:

> *This man, who will never be parted from me,*
> *kissed me on my mouth all trembling . . .*
> *That day we read no further . . .*

La bocca mi basciò tutto tremante, Francesca says, the quivering Paolo kisses her right on the lips. That's as close to medieval erotica as we're likely to get. The seemingly perfect, polite Francesca utters words that would never leave the mouth of a well-bred lady. What's more, she is unrepentant: in Dante's hell, the sinners would have you believe that it's never *their* fault—it's always someone else's.

In a tour de force of showing over telling, Dante gives Francesca just enough verbal rope to hang herself.

Francesca's plight has confounded readers for centuries. How could Dante punish her for doing only what comes naturally—for pursuing what is often best in us, the part that loses itself in love? To punish lust is one thing—but shouldn't true love earn a divine pass? In condemning Francesca, many readers believe, Dante is attacking love. A kindred soul of the lustful in *Inferno* 5, the poet Byron became so obsessed with Francesca that he made a pilgrimage to Rimini looking for traces of her. "But tell me, in the season of sweet sighs, / By what and how thy love to passion rose," he writes in his gorgeous translation of Dante's words to Francesca. You can feel Francesca's breath on his shoulders as he writes. Modern poetry's love god meets Dante's greatest lover.

Locked forever in their love, Francesca and Paolo are an indivisible pair. But their reward is damnation. Even worse, these lovers lack the one thing that makes passion possible: the body. They float through the afterlife like two weeping doves—condemned to a love that is not physical. Trying to love each other without a body.

Trattando, Dante would write, *l'ombre come cosa salda.*

Treating shades as solid things.

That's a challenge of life in the Underworld: accepting that the beloved ghost you burn for is no longer flesh and blood. And accepting that your conversation with the dead is actually a monologue, a love letter never to reach its destination.

ONE WEEK AFTER ISABEL'S BIRTH, I brought her home from the hospital with my sisters, Margaret, Mary, Rose, and Tina. We drove in separate cars, a Calabrian funeral procession incongruously transporting a new life. On the way back we went to lunch at a local diner, where I ordered the Cobb salad, just as I had many times with Katherine. The day was supposed to have been the happiest of our life. Instead, I was sitting in a dingy restaurant with my four sisters, eating wilted leaves. At home waiting was not my beautiful wife, but my seventy-six-year-old Calabrian mother, Yolanda—who now kept her false teeth in an empty glass on the bathroom sink, in the spot where Katherine had left her Deruta mug.

After her eight days in the neonatal unit, Isabel now weighed four pounds and seven ounces.

"She's ready to go now," the chief pediatrician had told me the day before.

I stared at him speechless.

"But . . ." I finally muttered, "wouldn't she be safer here?" I thought of all the whirring and beeping machines surrounding Isabel with antiseptic indifference and knew, in my terrified heart, the answer.

"The hospital's no place for healthy babies," he said smiling. "Your daughter's fine."

Although she was six weeks premature, Isabel had indeed faced down all the dangers posed by her extraordinary birth— first and foremost, the impact of the accident. The paramedics found Katherine hunched over her belly as if to protect her child. In the transition from the womb to the world, Isabel was denied oxygen as Katherine's brain shut down, and the doctors were concerned that this might affect the baby's own developing brain. But again, Isabel came through with surprising normalcy. After her revival through intubation, she was voracious, alert, breathing—everything that a newborn baby should be, although in a tiny package. Still, the idea of bringing her home frightened me. She was no bigger than a loaf of bread, and I didn't know the first thing about caring for a baby—let alone one that weighed less than five pounds. The head nurse could sense my naked fear. She took extra time to detail all the things I would need to do while Isabel was under my care, but the cascading items on her list overwhelmed me. It was impossible for me to concentrate. I made her repeat the routines several times the morning that we left, a cold December day whose air, I imagined, would shock the hard-won equilibrium of Isabel's vital signs. Bundling her in extra layers of heavy blanket, I said good-bye to her team of doctors and nurses and made my way to the car park abutting Vassar Brothers Hospital, which stood two miles from Saint Francis Hospital, where Isabel had been born and her mother died.

And then we went home.

Katherine and I had set up Isabel's crib in our bedroom. We had wanted her sex to be a surprise, so there was no predominance of either blue or pink in the piles of baby clothes we had amassed. A few days before the accident, my family gave Katherine a baby shower in Rhode Island over the Thanksgiving holiday, lavishing us with boxes of linens, bottles, and bibs that were now stacked over my volumes of Petrarch and Leopardi.

Back from the diner, I laid Isabel down gently on a blue and white blanket that my aged neighbor, Carmela DeSantis, had given to my mother to celebrate my birth. My daughter lay sleeping on her mother's side of the bed. The joy of hearing Isabel's newborn breath struggled to break through the grief that was pulling all my emotions into a vacuum, leaving me numb and empty—beyond love. I wanted to be elated, to feel connected to my child. But a wrecking ball had smashed the beams connecting me to my natural world, crushing the bond between father and daughter into the same pile of rubble that was filled with the other remains of my life with Katherine. I took Isabel's tiny hand in my own. Even in miniature, I could see the tapering outline of Katherine's long elegant fingers. Isabel had my clump of dark hair and full features on the fair skin she had inherited from her mother—a chiaroscuro baby mixing shadow and light.

"They'll probably turn brown," a nurse in the neonatal unit had told me, pointing to Isabel's blue eyes, and I imagined how, soon enough, all vestiges of her mother would fade from this Italianate child. But there was a fine shape to the head that was Katherine's and not mine, and her slender, elongated body was also a miniaturized form of her mother's. I felt a rational love for the hand I held and stroked, but nothing instinctual and visceral. I was a ghost haunting what had been my own life.

Later that day, my sisters had to return to their husbands and jobs, while my mother remained in Tivoli with Isabel and me. From that day forward my mom did the bulk of the diaper changing, bottle feeding, babysitting, and other double-barreled chores that go into child care. That left me time to walk in the snow and mark up my dog-eared edition of *The Divine Comedy*, which I had taken to reading aloud to myself, the poem's soothing sounds one of the few things that could calm me. Meanwhile, my colleagues taught my classes for me while I went on leave for the final few weeks of the semester.

"Just leave Isabel with us and pick her up when she's sixteen," my sister Margaret joked before returning to Rhode Island. She was only partly kidding. Katherine had made it clear to me that she wanted to be a stay-at-home mother, while I would roam free to hunt my academic woolly mammoths. Now I was about to relinquish Katherine's maternal role to a phalanx of capable Calabrian matrons: my sisters commandeered by *generalissima* Yolanda Luzzi. She had six children and, with Isabel, thirteen grandchildren. Now, at the age of seventy-six, she was becoming a mother once again.

After a month of this new routine, classes ended for the holiday break. I made a second fateful decision that followed the grief-struck logic of my earlier decision to enlist my family in raising Isabel: I would move back to Rhode Island with my mom and Isabel and make our base there, while coming to Bard and Tivoli only on the few days each week I needed to teach, Tuesday to Thursday, a commute of roughly 175 miles each way. When I told my college president my plan, he had one word for it: harebrained. I also asked him that day if he believed in the eternal life of the soul. I was now anguishing over this question to which I had never given a second thought before.

The idea that Katherine was utterly and completely no more, in spirit as well as in flesh, tormented me after I saw her body for the last time at her funeral in Detroit, when I was shown her open casket before the mass in her parents' church. I stood in the room with her mother and father as well as her siblings, all of us there to say our final goodbyes. My sleek wife was now puffy and embalmed, all the definition gone from her features. I tried desperately to find her somewhere in there, to feel some communion as I held her hand and caressed her skin for the last time. But her forehead was as cold as marble when I kissed it, and I swore to her that I would protect and nurture our daughter, and that she, Katherine, would be a living presence for our little girl. But there was nothing left of the person I had loved in that body—that corpse in a red dress. If Katherine was anywhere in this universe, it had to be in some other form.

The fog of grief had descended on me, and I couldn't see the sense of my college president's words when he called my plan harebrained. I needed only to feel comforted by my family's love for me and our collective love for my new daughter. So, on December 23, 2007, I packed up my Tivoli apartment and drove with Isabel and my mother back to my hometown.

"You will leave behind everything you love." During Dante's exile, a scholar from Bologna offered him the title of poet laureate, but he respectfully declined. Only if one day Florence asks me back as its honored poet, he said, then I'll accept and return victorious to my sheepfold, my *bello ovile*.

I had returned to the sheepfold of my childhood, but the soft *L* sounds of Dante's twin words could not calm my racing heart, no matter how many times I read aloud the passage about his exile.

THERE IS NO LOVE THAT IS NOT PHYSICAL.

You learn this when you're faced with the sudden death of your beloved.

From the time that the nine-year-old Dante first laid eyes on an eight-year-old Florentine girl named Beatrice Portinari in 1274, you can just imagine him holding the syllables of her nickname on his tongue: *BEE-chay*. When he saw her again, nine years later, Bice had become a woman. In all likelihood, he had seen her in the interim, but the book he wrote about their unusual love story, the *Vita Nuova*, needed something more symbolic to drive the narrative. So Beatrice became her full name, the "thrice-blessed one"—just like the Trinity, the holy number three that, when squared, gave Dante the magical number nine.

When Dante was eighteen, he had a Francesca da Rimini moment: Beatrice came to him in a dream, naked except for a crimson and white cloth draped around her. She was sleeping, carried in the arms of the God of Love. The imposing figure, who went by his Latin name Amor, was brandishing something in flames. He announced to Dante: *Vide cor tuum*. Behold your heart. Then Amor woke up the sleeping Beatrice, who proceeded to eat the burning heart. It was Dante's.

This vision of the burning heart incited Dante to write a sonnet. He circulated it among the leading poets of Florence, none of whom could understand it (one, a doctor, told Dante to wash his testicles in cold water to calm himself). There was one who got it, however: Guido Cavalcanti, like Beatrice a richer and better-connected Florentine whom Dante regarded with a mixture of adoration and jealousy. Guido was the unofficial leader of the Sweet New Style, the poetic movement that spoke of love as a lacerating illness that elevated the soul but destroyed the body. Guido immediately responded with a sonnet of his own to Dante: "I think that you beheld all goodness," he wrote of Dante's terrifying vision.

Guido's poem made it official: Dante was now accepted into the Sweet New Style, beginning his career as a Florentine poet.

But Dante's Beatrice, unlike other Sweet New Style muses, actually had a personality. She was no mere object of worship— someone lovely to look at but impossible to know. When Beatrice saw Dante paying too much attention to his *donna-schermo*, the "screen lady" whom he pretended to love so as to hide his feelings for Beatrice, she refused to greet him in the street. No other Sweet New Style woman would have shamed her poet like this. Dante was different from his fellow poets in other ways. He addressed a poem about Beatrice to *Donne ch'avete intelletto di amore*, "Ladies who have knowledge of love," choosing female readers over the typical male audience. He saw women as more than just beautiful bodies.

Then, at the center of the *Vita Nuova*, the beautiful witch-ladies with the crazy hair tell Dante that he too will die, and that Beatrice has gone to the other side. He woke up to find it was all a dream. Or was it? Soon after his vision, Dante writes, Beatrice dies. Florence is now a widower; Dante is a widower—to a woman who was never his wife. And indeed, the real-life Beatrice Portinari died on June 8, 1290, at age twenty-four.

The strangest thing in the *Vita Nuova*, perhaps in all of Dante's career, happens next. Instead of expressing his grief, he writes that when Beatrice died, the heavens aligned in a symbol of perfect holiness. In his sadness, he tried to transform Beatrice into one of those angelic, interchangeable, and ultimately forgettable, Sweet New Style muses. After all, had his fellow poets faced her death, they would have moved on quickly to another muse and found another body to love once Beatrice's was gone.

Or maybe idealizing her was a survival mechanism for Dante, a reflexive turn to some familiar and reassuring way of explaining Beatrice's devastating loss.

Either way, the plan breaks down. Dante's grief is unrelenting, and he mopes around the city of Florence, too distracted to write poetry, too heartbroken to hide his sorrow. His fellow poets, especially Cavalcanti, tell him *basta*, enough is enough: excessive mourning is unnatural; even worse, it's vulgar. *Volgare*. Time to move on. Write about another woman, they tell him. Find another body to love.

We read in the *Vita Nuova* that, a year after Beatrice's death, Dante finds himself in the center of Florence among the city's leading citizens. I picture him sitting with a paintbrush, drawing an angel, oblivious to the commotion in the piazza.

"Someone was with me just now," he tells a passerby who stops to look at his picture, "that's why I was so deep in thought."

Then I see him pick up his brush and walk away—an hour with the angels is all he can take.

Soon afterward, in the midst of his drawing and despair, he sees a pretty face and all the promise it holds. She takes pity on Dante, he reads it in her eyes and wonders: maybe she can replace Beatrice. His poetry takes aim at her, his verses bursting with grateful tears. This *donna gentile*, gentle lady, was looking at Dante from a window above him, beckoning him to fall in love again. Dante understood that the logical, even natural thing to do would be to give himself over to this gentle lady and leave Beatrice to her early, unfortunate grave. Let her die in peace. Then he has a vision, a miraculous vision. Beatrice appears to him dressed in that same crimson and white cloth that draped her figure when she devoured Dante's burning heart. Suddenly, Dante is riven with shame. How could he have even considered taking up with the beautiful lady in the window? No, he would devote his feelings—and his poetry—to the blessed Beatrice. The *Vita Nuova* ends with Dante promising silence: he will only write again when he is capable of describing Beatrice in a fitting way. First, he says, he must study.

Long study and great love—the same words that would bring Dante to Virgil in the dark wood, and that would bring me to Dante in my time of greatest woe.

JUST BEFORE I RETURNED TO Rhode Island, my editor at the university press that was about to publish my first book asked me if I could handle editing the final proofs of my manuscript. The book, *Romantic Europe and the Ghost of Italy*, was a study of the myth of Italy and its pull on foreign exiles such as Byron, that worshiper of Francesca da Rimini. It had taken me ten years to write the book, ever since I began my dissertation in the cement and steel of a library carrel filled with hundreds of books on Dante when I was a graduate student. I said yes to my editor. I would let nothing derail my career—that was the gauntlet I threw in the face of tragedy.

Back in Westerly, Rhode Island, with Isabel and my mother, I spent hours alone each day with the page proofs in an apartment I had rented a few minutes' drive from my mom's, checking citations, eliminating adverbs, and shortening footnotes. The mechanical work gave me the thing I desperately needed: solitude. Grinding away on my manuscript with pencil and eraser, vetting my words so meticulously that it must have shocked even my editor, I squirreled myself away for hours at a stretch. Meanwhile, I had outsourced the one job that could have given me a new home: being a father to Isabel.

In her new Westerly home, Isabel would sleep with her arms flung backward and her lips slightly open, a pose of absolute surrender to an unknown world. Like all babies, she was helpless, and yet she did not look like other babies, with that girlish fineness to her features and searching gaze. I don't know what, if anything, she was looking for, and I couldn't help but trace her sight line out toward Katherine, the natural mother she had been separated from forever. My daughter's baby smell, its mix of powder, formula, and new skin, would melt me, and I was astonished by her newborn beauty. But my thoughts were too busy following Isabel's gaze into Katherine's absence for any of these sights, smells, and sounds to break grief's hermetic seal.

No matter how many diapers I changed, or how much baby spittle fell on my collar, I didn't feel like a real dad. Part of me was elsewhere. Obsessed with my work. Dreaming of a new home. Speaking with the dead. Kicking at the sandy beaches of my Rhode Island exile. And sounding Dante's rhyming tercets over and over, as if they were a charm to ward off evil spirits.

After editing all day, I would return to my mother's house and play with Isabel for a while before my mom fed her and got her ready for bed. Then, after reading or watching television, I would go to sleep in my high school bed across the hall from my daughter's room. Katherine's death had sent me into the dark wood, a new dimension of life that I had never imagined existed. And now, having fallen into that other life, I had splintered off into the most bizarre realm of all: my childhood, which I was reinhabiting as a forty-year-old. I knew that divorce and depression could send grown men back in broken heaps to the homes they had grown up in. I did not expect as much from death. But there I was, watching *Hannity and Colmes* on Fox, in my pajamas and on my mother's rust-colored sofa, my feet on her red shag carpeting, the stillness of her dead-end street as impenetrable as the fog that had descended upon me. I was supposed to be taking care of a baby, but now I needed to be taken care of, and I had returned to the safest place I knew.

At around three a.m. Isabel's cries would often echo throughout the hallway. I would awake to them, prop my head against the pillow for a moment, and then pad across the hallway to where my mother would already be holding Isabel in her arms. "*Lassa jera, ci penzo io,*" she would say as I loitered by the crib. "Leave her be, I'll take care of it." Usually I would demur, sliding past my mother and Isabel and retreating to my bed and fetal sleep.

But one night, for no reason other than the faint call of that same instinct that had otherwise abandoned me, I awoke with a start as Isabel's sobs sent me running to the crib.

"*Dai, lascia stare, ci penso io,*" I answered in standard Italian to her Calabrian dialect. "Let go please, I've got her."

My mother scurried off, half in worry that I would drop or mishandle or fail to quiet Isabel, half that I was losing precious sleep when I needed to get my strength back. Ours was not a house where grown men held crying babies at night.

As I held the chaos of my hysterical baby in the dead of that winter night, I imagined the impact between Katherine's jeep and the oncoming van, the crunching of metal and explosion of debris along the narrow country road. Isabel's actual screams merged with Katherine's imaginary ones, signaling to me that the world was fundamentally a place of disorder and violence. It was a constant reminder that I hadn't been able to save my wife, that I might not be able to protect my daughter. The ill-fated turns, the undertows, the black ice, the live wires—they were everywhere.

Seven hundred years earlier, in the throes of his doomed youthful love for Beatrice, Dante too sensed the fragility of life when he dreamed of the ladies with wild hair and their menacing words. Dante intuited his vision as an omen, a sign that his love for Beatrice was star-crossed. Now that the heavens had indeed misaligned in my own life I could not get Dante's fateful syllables with their rolling *R*'s out of my head. *Tu pur morrai.*

Isabel wasn't crying out of fear or for her mother at three a.m. But I heard them as fear or longing. My rational mind understood that she blessedly knew nothing of these sentiments, yet her cries gave voice to my own anguish. I was in charge of protecting her, but it was my mother who spent her days holding my daughter in her arms. Grief had compromised my sense of other people's needs, even my daughter's—the bundle of life I was now cradling and comforting, our two hearts pounding as we clung to each other, both of us desperate for the human touch as we rode the arrow shot by exile's bow, neither of us knowing if and where it would ever land.

CHAPTER 2

Consider Your Seed

I wasn't the only one eviscerated by Katherine's death. She was unlike the other women I had brought home to meet my family. She did not have a fancy college degree or silver nose ring; she knew not a single band of alternative music or misunderstood, avant-garde foreign filmmaker, as Katherine's tastes ran toward the all-American and wholesome, from Top-40 pop to Ellen DeGeneres stand-up comedy. The coeds from the Rhode Island School of Design and Oberlin and fissured nuclear families had rankled my mother and sisters with their arch comments and indifferent hygiene. They regarded my family as loveable Martians, quaintly inscrutable creatures beholden to passé virtues like marital fidelity and the severest home economics. In Katherine, my family finally had someone who did not disdain big-box retailers and suburban raised ranch houses. She was a woman without irony, the slightest tinge of snark.

"Joe, I really hope you don't screw this one up," my younger sister, Tina, had said to me the first time she met Katherine. Her look was as grave as her tone of voice: this could be a grown-up relationship, her eyes suggested, you've had your fun; now get real.

Mogli e buoi dei paesi tuoi, the Italian expression goes—wife and oxen from your hometown. Katherine was from my metaphysical village.

A few years before I met Katherine, I had been engaged in graduate school to a brilliant woman who promised me a life I had dreamed of, a world of affluence and high culture, everything I had lacked growing up. The night after passing my oral PhD exams, I met Amanda for the first time in an Ethiopian restaurant just off campus. Her graceful gentleness and guileless blue eyes, framed by wire glasses, arrested me. The next morning, in rough shape from a night of celebrating, I made a point of waking up early to hear her eight thirty a.m. paper on Brazilian history; within a few months we were basically living together, editing each other's papers, planning trips on graduate student stipends to her parents' properties in London, Saint Croix, and Princeton. One night, her father, a vigorous bon vivant who had built a thriving law practice, took us to a restaurant near his home in New Brunswick, New Jersey.

"Try the python," he prodded, "or the kangaroo."

The exotic menu was filled with the wildest game, and as I stared across the table at Amanda the world felt like an endless banquet of all the foods I could never have imagined or afforded. She was taking me to a new village, one far from the one where I had grown up in Rhode Island, and it was filled with kindness, respect, and love. I ordered the kangaroo.

In 2000, two months after receiving my doctorate and three years into our time together, I asked Amanda to marry me on the beaches of Watch Hill, the wooden carousel cresting on the horizon behind her. In tears, she said yes. I didn't tell her that I had only bought the ring the day before, and that I had been wracked with doubt on the walk to the jeweler, a trip I had taken after months of wavering. Something deep inside me was saying, *Stop, don't do this*. I tried nonetheless to love Amanda the way that she deserved, and I felt like a fool for even thinking of giving up the magical possibilities that life with her held. But my admiration and affection for her refused to blossom into true love. As the wedding approached, my misgivings began to manifest themselves in petty remarks and outbursts, as though I were goading her into fights that she knew neither of us believed in. Perhaps she could sense my ambivalence, and it made her usually low-key self become tetchy and irritable. Soon enough we were fighting nonstop. I became annoyed at how, in the manner of academic liberals, she found so many things "offensive" or "unjust," even though she had benefited from American capitalism in every conceivable way. She began to lose patience with the company I kept: guys like me, laddish and uncouth boys who had not spent their lives in the polished worldly institutions that had been the air she breathed. The day we went to pick out our wedding invitations—a tasteful but outrageously expensive medley of sylvan designs on heavily bonded paper—we had a blowout fight over nothing in particular.

"What's happening to us?" she asked.

"Are we making a mistake?" I replied.

That April, six weeks before our wedding and with the invitations already mailed out, we called things off.

A thought flashed across my mind that first night in the hospital after Katherine's death. I would go home, back to my metaphysical village, to the place where more than any other I could be myself, with no need to impress—a longing Katherine understood viscerally. Katherine and I were both a bit lost in the new lives we'd chosen and the comfort of familiarity we'd left behind. I missed my home state, its beaches and weather-beaten shingles, the old-world wealth and new-world eccentricity. "Welcome to Rhode Island," I recall our longtime cartoonist Don Bosquet writing, "where we can pronounce 'Quonochontaug' and 'Misquamicut' but can't say 'chow-duh' [chowder]." I had left the state at eighteen, one of the few from my high school to venture out of South County, as most of my classmates landed at the nearby University of Rhode Island (URI, or Ewe-Ah-Eye in the local accent). Part of me was envious. The frat houses and keg stands of URI, the house parties in

Bonnet Shores, the surfers with ropey bracelets and suntanned athletic girls with long limbs—I would know none of this in my bookish world. The turf farms and ocean breezes surrounding the local college seemed to promise a simpler life.

Katherine had been suffering from a similar homesickness. She was never fully at ease in our college town and missed her family in Michigan, the Midwestern sincerity, the strong Republican values of her father and his political circles. I could feel the tension radiate from her at dinner parties as friends of ours, over couscous and ciabatta, excoriated Cheney and Rumsfeld. She knew that she could not speak her mind in these circles. And she knew that I disagreed with her on almost all political matters. But I had learned to live with our opposing viewpoints and even found it exhilarating to hear her tell me, in private, why she rejected the principles governing my world. The part of me that had grown up in a blue-collar family light-years from the liberal chatter of the ivory tower also relished her unabashed embrace of the family values and enterprising spirit that had helped my own family climb out of centuries of Calabrian squalor and make it into the American middle class.

The morning of her accident, she had been driving to the State University of New York at New Paltz for a final exam in one of her humanities courses. She had a 3.75 grade point average and was majoring in history, after having been accepted into the college's honors program the year before. But she was struggling to balance her pregnancy, her work as a Pilates instructor, and her life in a world far from her family in Michigan and actor friends in New York. At the end of the day, there were term papers to write and oral reports to prepare for, but there was no clear sense of where it was all heading, as she had not decided what—if any—career she wanted for her post-acting life. And then there were all those brainiacs to deal with. Once in North Carolina she told one of the fellows at the Humanities Center, a well-known Slavic poet, that she hated the film *Pulp Fiction* because it was, in her words, "immoral." She certainly could have chosen a more politic term, but that was just how she was: transparent, emotional, direct, not given to abstractions and open-ended arguments. The poet gave her a vacant, confused look. My wife was breaking a sacred rule of the chattering classes: never make an unsubtle point about a major cultural phenomenon. And never hold art to the same standards as life. I wonder how he would have reacted if he found out her dirtiest secret of all: this lithe, artsy Midwestern girl was a dyed-in-the-wool *Republican*.

Unlike Katherine's, my own career path had been a clearly defined one, even when I briefly stepped off it for some fun as a bartender or backpacker in Europe. Her return to college seemed logical enough to me: she was smart, would do well, and would get a decent job for her efforts. I wanted to have my domestic cake, with Katherine as stay-at-home mom, and eat it too, with her also going out and earning some money in a job that wouldn't overly tax or distract her. *Please, God, just let her earn $50,000 a year,* I prayed, sometimes loud enough for Katherine to hear. I never imagined a life of financial hardship for us, not after all those years of study and sacrifice. Faced with the reality of our one-income household and my modest professorial salary, I began to increase the pressure on Katherine.

"Honey, just aim for something steady," my typical harangue would go, "something more than a few hours of Pilates here and there."

Shortly after moving to North Carolina, we went shopping on a gorgeous September day. We separated for a bit and made plans to meet at the car. A half hour after our appointed time, Katherine bounced over, apologizing for being late, but happily clutching a bag full of expensive cosmetics. My worry at her lateness turned to anger and I started shouting at her, asking where she'd been and why she hadn't answered my calls. I said that we couldn't afford the two hundred dollars of facial creams and exfoliants, that she had to change her ways and handle money better.

"You need to make some instead of just spending it!" I cried.

She burst into tears. I had struck a nerve in Katherine much deeper than her questionable home economics. Ever since renouncing acting, she had been trying to recover from the loss of her youthful dreams. Now, in her thirties, she feared that what she imagined to be her greatest gift, her beauty, which she had relied upon her entire life, would one day fade. The cosmetics were a cry for help—a plea I mistook for vanity. Instead of intuiting her needs, I made it about my fears of not being able to provide fully for her and our family. Katherine needed a loving word, and instead I played the part of the perfect brute, ruining a beautiful sunny day just as we were starting our life together.

Katherine was a dreamer—we both were, except that, unlike mine, her dreams weren't tethered to the icy logic of credentials and connections. She lived in the moment, a place I rarely visited. This is why I had fallen in love with her. This is also why our otherwise happy relationship could plague me with worry about our future together.

My decision that first night in the hospital to move back "home"—I still used the word to describe my hometown of Westerly, even though I hadn't truly lived there since high school—was partly because Katherine and I had felt so comfortable there as a couple. When she spent time with my family, Katherine experienced none of the tension and insecurity that rankled her when she was with my colleagues and academic friends. Loving Katherine had enabled me to reconnect to the person that I had been when I was growing up. I had spent years trying to smother my Rhode Island accent ("How fah from the pahk ah we?"). But when I had a bit to drink, or when I woke up first thing in the morning, the *R* would instinctively fade into *H*. I was a Luzzi, after all, Westerly High class of '85, no matter how far I traveled away from the South County coast or how many degrees I collected. To understand how far I had tried to run from Westerly before circling back, all you had to do was ask my name. For years I had been pronouncing it differently from my family, preferring the Italianized "LOO-tsie" to their staunchly American "luz-zy" (rhymes with "fuz-zy"). As they were trying to assimilate to their new American life, I insisted on reclaiming legendary Calabria, looking for an Italianate pronunciation to distinguish myself. On paper, I had the same name as my mother and sisters—but I had taken to announcing it differently to the world, to show how much distance I had placed between my point of origin and myself.

A FEW WEEKS AFTER MOVING to Westerly I idled in the parking lot of a downtown bookstore, listening to an audiobook of Homer's *Odyssey*, with the gravelly voice of Ian McKellen as Odysseus. I needed stories to get me through the long days in my hometown. I drove around for hours with the CD playing, skirting the coast and avoiding my mother, my sisters, and the fortress they were building around Isabel. I parked by the beaches and stopped to look out into the surf, listening to McKellen narrate how Odysseus negotiated one obstacle after another on his way back to Ithaca from the Trojan war. A seagull landed near my car and gutted a crab; Odysseus wandered while his wife, Penelope, waited, spinning wool and fending off suitors. Katherine had only been gone a few months, and I was back in the Calabrian bosom that I had left behind as a teenager, when I was determined to leave my Italian American immigrant world and never return. I was also back to teaching at Bard, doing all I could to remain connected to the college community that had closed ranks around me, just as my family had, to help me make it through the Underworld in one piece. McKellen continued his tale of Odysseus's winding journey, splitting the waves of the Aegean and plowing its foam as he hurried in the direction of a home that had been entirely transformed, crowded with gluttonous and conniving suitors hoping to win Penelope's hand.

"The queenly nymph [Calypso] sought out the great Odysseus," McKellen spoke, "and found him there on the headland, sitting, still, / weeping, his eyes never dry, his sweet life flowing away / with the tears he wept for his foiled journey home."

Odysseus looked out to sea by Calypso's cave, tears streaming from him like summer rain over the Aegean. Calypso was a stunning sea nymph who had taken Odysseus prisoner and fallen in love with him, fulfilling his every desire but one: the irrepressible need he felt to return to his homeland. I had made it back to Westerly, my Ithaca. But when I drove along the coast, walked through the historic downtown, and ran along the beach, I felt as invisible as one of Dante's shades in the afterworld. I wasn't returning or revisiting the world of my childhood; I was haunting it.

I sat in my car for another hour, waiting for Odysseus's ship to make landfall. Meanwhile, the seagull abandoned the crab as the purple and orange dusk spread over the winter ocean, reminding me that it was time to return to Batterson Avenue, where my mother was warming bottles of Similac formula for Isabel's dinner.

WE MEET DANTE'S ULISSE—FOR ULYSSES, the Roman form of Homer's Greek hero Odysseus—in Malebolge, a moral black hole consisting of ten concentric ditches toward the bottom of Inferno. According to Dante, the farther you get from God's love, the colder it gets, so the pit of Inferno is all ice. And the deeper one goes into Dante's hell, the smarter the sinners. In Malebolge, the greatest holding pit of human evil in the universe, the sin of fraud is punished. The previous sins in hell, including the lust of Paolo and Francesca, were failures of will, as the body's appetites overwhelmed the mind that was supposed to constrain them. But in Malebolge the sinners abuse a greater gift than the body: here the intellect has turned sour.

Throughout *The Divine Comedy*, Dante engages in intense conversations with his characters, from the sinners in hell to the blessed in heaven. Most everyone he meets, including the eloquent chatterbox Francesca da Rimini, talks Dante's ear off, as they desperately recount how they had been wronged or how they had been saved. Everyone except Ulysses. He is unapproachable. Transformed into a tongue of flame, he hisses words at a starstruck Dante, who listens but doesn't dare speak back, heeding Virgil's words that the great Greek hero might hold him in scorn.

In Homer's epic telling, Odysseus endured ten years of war in Troy, then ten years of wandering through the wine-dark waters separating him from his island of Ithaca and his wife, Penelope. But nothing could stop him from returning home. He ran a spike through the eye of the drunken Cyclops; he stopped his ears with wax against the song of the Sirens; he rescued his crew from the seductive drug of forgetfulness in the Land of the Lotus-eaters; he cried an Aegean Sea of protest against Calypso and her enticements. Homer's Odysseus embodies devotion to home; Dante's Ulysses is as restless as his flaming tongue, as he describes the overwhelming sense of displacement he felt upon returning to Ithaca:

neither fondness for my son, nor devotion
to my old father, nor the love I owed
Penelope that would have contented her,
could overcome the lust
I felt inside to become an expert
on the world's vices and its virtues.

Nothing can calm Ulysses' yearning soul: he burns to return to the high seas and his wanderer's life. He convenes a meeting with his former comrades, asking them to join him in leaving Ithaca and setting sail for new adventures.

Remember, he tells them: "you were not made to live like brutes, / but to pursue virtue and knowledge."

They succumb to his magical words and rush to join him at sea. But their joy soon turns to fright. Within a fortnight, a terrible storm strikes their vessel. No honeyed words can save them now. The sea closes over them—*"com' altrui piacque,"* Dante writes, "as pleased another," implying that the heavens were not on Ulysses' side.

Francesca made Dante wonder: how do you love a person without a body—when you are so heartbroken that you can't imagine her alive anymore? Ulysses' lesson is even more bitter: once you lose your former life—to use that wooden term—you can never get it back. In a complete reversal of Homer, Dante sends Ulysses back to sea after he has returned home—because the home he finds back in Ithaca is no longer home.

AS I GAZED OUT TO the Atlantic and listened to McKellen narrate the *Odyssey*, I pictured Dante's Ulysses coming home to Ithaca and created my own version of the story, just as Dante had. In my telling, Ulysses' tale went like this:

In the twenty years since he had left his wife, Ulysses had known other women and he had wept a sea of tears. Yet he had forsaken all of them, human and divine, for this very moment. He had made it back to the home he was born in. He was standing in his bedroom—the place where he had left the things of childhood and later slept as a man. His hair stood on end. Nothing had changed: the rooms were filled with everything he had left behind. And there it was, in the center of the room, the bed on a platform of a massive oak tree trunk. He took the sheets in his arms: they smelled of sandalwood and soap.

He smelled his wife on the sheets, for the first time in twenty years. His pulse raced: they were finally together in the same house, and within hours he would smell her flesh and touch her skin. He would make love to the wife who had become a woman without a body—a perfect, remote shadow in his dreams and daydreams.

He had killed countless rivals (and was about to slaughter his wife's suitors), had matched wits with the most brilliant, and crossed swords with the most ferocious. He had lived in

Calypso's cave for seven years, captive to a jealous lover who provided him with everything he could ever hope for, but did not want. Amid the nymphs wreathed in seaweed, the suckling pigs, and the writhing dancers, he would wander to a clump of rocks that jutted out into the sea. And he would weep, rivers of tears that soaked his tunic and splashed against the stone. All the while, he stared in the direction of the house that smelled of sandalwood and soap.

Now he had made it home.

The sandalwood and soap filled his body, first with sweetness.

Then with nausea.

Back in my own childhood home after twenty years—falling asleep on my mom's living room sofa while Sean Hannity and Alan Colmes duked it out over gun control and health care—I could feel Ulysses' nausea in the pit of my stomach.

Nausea: that's the sensation Dante used to describe his exile, which he said teaches you *"come sa di sale / lo pane altrui"*—"how salty is the taste / of another man's bread." He wasn't waxing metaphorical: they have made bread without salt in Florence from Dante's time until today, and nothing reminds a Florentine more of home than this desalinated staple.

A FEW MONTHS INTO MY stay in Westerly, I returned to Katherine's hometown outside Detroit to celebrate her father's retirement from the bench. The day I arrived, her parents and I drove to the cemetery on a rainy day similar to the one when we had buried Katherine months earlier. That night, her father gave his farewell speech to hundreds of power brokers at the Oakland Hills Country Club, a site that has hosted the U.S. Open golf championships. He ended his talk by clapping for the audience, saying that the applause should be for them, not him, and many cried, partly because they were inspired by his words, partly because of the pity they felt for him, for me seated beside him, and for Isabel back in Rhode Island with her *nonna*. I looked around the table as he spoke. Katherine's mother had aged beyond recognition. More than anyone else, she could not accept what happened. At first, she didn't react to the news. At the hospital in Poughkeepsie the day after Katherine died she showed up making small talk, even cracking jokes.

"I can't believe that kid is gone," she kept repeating, but there were no tears, only a faraway look in her eyes. We all knew it wasn't because she didn't care—it was because she cared too much. A husband who loses his wife may one day have the chance to rebuild, perhaps even get a second chance at happiness. A parent gets no such reprieve. The sight of Katherine's parents standing by their daughter's grave brought to mind Virgil's description of the families in the Underworld, harrowing words that Dante knew by heart:

mothers and grown men and ghosts of great-souled heroes,
their bodies stripped of life, and boys and unwed girls
and sons laid on the pyre before their parents' eyes.

I felt no connection to the mossy patch where Katherine's body lay in Royal Oak Cemetery. The facticity—now there's an ugly word—of death was all I found. My tears didn't even feel genuine. I knew I was supposed to cry and so, *bravo ragazzo*, clever boy, that I was, I played the part of the grieving husband to a T. Her parents—fine, broken people who would never recover, who had abandoned all hope—also wept, streaming frightening tears and groans that seemed to emanate, raw and animal-like, from the pit of their stomachs. Their daughter had been returned to her people. But this expanse of stones, flags, and flowers meant nothing to me. I was still numb from the shock of Katherine's sudden death. She was like a phantom limb, the pain of something not there. Worse still, guilt ravaged my insides, as I felt as though I had failed my wife and this kindly couple. *Their daughter died on my watch*, I had said to Georgia. I said the right things to whoever would listen—and there were many caring people who paused to hear—about how I missed her, how she lived on in our daughter. But the purifying tears would not flow, as I turned inward, home only inside Dante's verses or the long walks I took alone in my upstate village, on icy streets as bereft of life as the frozen lakes of Inferno.

I needed help—more help than any priest could give. I had no clue how to love somebody without a body, and so I reached out to another great-souled woman.

"I'M TRYING TO HOLD IT together," I said to my grief counselor, Rosalind, at the start of our first meeting. Her office was in a nondescript development off coastal Route 1, about an hour from my mom's house in Westerly. I had deliberately chosen someplace far enough from home to ensure that I wouldn't be recognized. In my macho Calabrian culture, a man was expected to keep his problems locked inside, not bare them to a stranger, however qualified. For a man like my father, confession was something you did before a priest, in the privacy of the confessional, and psychoanalysis was for sissies. Other than my family, the only people who knew I was getting help of this kind were the anonymous patients I passed by in Rosalind's waiting room before and after my appointments. But we understood the rules and never made eye contact.

Trying not to look like a broken-down soul, I wore a striped oxford shirt and wide-wale cords. After a few minutes of conversation, it was clear that, like my chaplain Georgia, Rosalind was put on earth to help others. I had never known such people until Katherine died. My family had granted me unusual kindnesses, but that was a primal, Casa Luzzi thing, decidedly intramural. Living with my tyrannical father, getting by with very little, inheriting Calabrian reservoirs of *la miseria*—it had all made these Batterson Avenue women tough and pragmatic. They saw life as a struggle and acted accordingly.

Like Georgia, Rosalind was schooled in the love of humanity. She had become a mother at a young age, raised well-adjusted and high-achieving children, and chosen her career for karma, not profit. That first meeting she told me it was too soon to try and get my life together and come to terms with what had happened. Too soon for everything. She was an earthy and capable Nordic woman, someone who could tend a large garden with strong hands. She was not sentimental, but she was emotional. My story got to her. I told her how and why I felt so guilty, that my not taking care of Isabel on my own was crushing me—and that I was caving under the weight of my family's aid.

"Why can't I do this on my own?" I asked.

"No, that's not right," Rosalind countered. "Isabel is getting the powerful love of a powerful family, exactly what she needs. And you are doing the best you can, under the circumstances."

That was the refrain we kept coming back to, her most dearly held belief: people do the best they can in the place and time in which they find themselves, which is all they are capable of, even if retrospection or detached analysis tells a different story. These were Rosalind's articles of faith: humans are essentially good and loving creatures. Sometimes that goodness and love become misdirected, but they are always there, driving the gears of the universe. Her creed, I would discover, was also Dante's—but that would come later. Much later.

In Rosalind's eyes, I was not who I feared I had become: a selfish careerist and calculating survivor, incapable of rising to the occasion and setting aside my own needs to raise my daughter. Instead, I was someone who was struggling to love himself again. Until I could do that, she believed, I would never love another human being—or be able to take care of one.

She sat and listened and told me that it was too soon—words that an impatient and striving nature like mine couldn't accept.

I couldn't hurry my grief along into mourning, nor could I find that middle ground between surrendering to my family and striking out on my own with Isabel. All the while, she tapped her clogs on the cushioned footrest, looking at me with understanding blue eyes for our fifty-five minutes, while my own brown eyes passed judgment on everything in sight, especially myself.

Back in Westerly, I was using up my share of goodwill with my family. I had been the golden child indulged since birth, so deep down I expected my mother and sisters to handle the more demanding aspects of childrearing. This freed me for jaunts to the playground with Isabel, vanilla ice cream with her on the beach, and father-daughter sing-alongs at the local music program. Professionally, I may have inhabited ultraliberal turf, but I had been raised according to the gender dictates of ancient Calabria. I grew up watching my mother tend to my father like an aide-de-camp; I would never have admitted as much, but to me it was taken for granted that my mother would change Isabel's diapers while I slept soundly.

With each midnight diaper changing that I slept through, with each afternoon nap I avoided by fleeing the house to play tennis or go work on my book, Isabel's infancy was slipping through my fingers. My mother was devoted to Isabel, but she was old and tired, and her regimen of feeding my daughter consisted of goods that you could pick up at the gas station: Lipton soup, Nabisco crackers, Kraft mac and cheese, and Jell-O pudding, all hangovers from my nutri-

tionally challenged childhood. I insisted on healthy and organic foods, but I let my mother and sisters do the shopping.
I bought the essentials, the diapers and the formula; but, in
my absence, I let the decisions for Isabel's day-to-day care
fall to them.

Isabel's diet was not the only rein I relinquished. Most
days, instead of taking Isabel with me to the park or to the
library, I let my sister Margaret bundle her up along with
her little cousins Michaela and Rosie and whisk her off to
the Crystal Mall in Waterford, Connecticut, where Isabel
would pass a spring afternoon riding a mechanical horse
by a food court or putting coins into a pinball machine at
nearby Chuck E. Cheese's. To stop these trips I would have
had to stop burying myself in my teaching and writing and
emerge from the protective barrier of footnotes I had erected
between the world and myself. Or I would have had to liqui-
date my puny savings and hire a child-care provider to help
me raise Isabel on my terms. But I balked and took the path
of least resistance.

My family thrilled to Isabel, and she to them. When I took
her out with me, to lunch to meet a friend visiting from Bard or
to the local Music Together along with the other yuppie prog-
eny, Isabel clung to me in desperate, awkward shyness. She
was out of her element, and longed to return to the warmth
and chaos of the Luzzi brood, with cousins climbing over one
another in a mad dash for potato chips and cupcakes, as the
soundtrack of the Mickey Mouse Clubhouse looped in perma-

nently. With the stalwart rotation of my mom and four sisters, Isabel was forever on a fresh round of play dates and fun, from the soft-serve ice cream at oceanside Dusty's to the thwacking pins at the Alley Katz Bowling Center. I had known and loved all these places growing up, but now this was *her* world, not mine, and I felt as though I were walking into a foreign country without the requisite visa each time I went to pick her up. She would smile at first when she saw me, but then start to fuss and eventually cry. Westerly was no land of exile for my daughter. It was the first place where she had known the love and camaraderie that made her infancy so happy, and made her a stranger to the tragedy that hung over her birth. Westerly was her home.

My family's help had freed me to pursue my interests and my career—yet, I told Rosalind, I was suffering severe guilt over this ancient Italian division of labor. Rosalind insisted that I was making a mistake.

"It's not so simple," she would answer. "It's not *either* you let your family raise Isabel, *or* you do it on your own."

I was making an intellectual error, she suggested, not to mention a moral one. *You're doing the best you can, under the circumstances,* she kept saying, but I found no comfort in her words. If I really needed to change the situation, she told me, I would find a way to do so.

I was living under the spell of what one author, Joan Didion, called magical thinking: the cool-minded craziness of those who expect their loved one back at any moment, ready to put on a familiar pair of old shoes. I knew that Katherine wasn't coming back for those knockout leopard-print shoes she wore the night I met her in Williamsburg. Mine was a different kind of magical thinking: the sense that the world began and ended with my own suffering. My grief became an airtight shell, and contrary to the calm outward appearance I cultivated, my sorrow now defined me. Grief was choking my imagination, leaving me incapable of envisioning a different life.

Worst of all, my sorrow was keeping me from forming an emotional attachment with Isabel. I loved her, but I did not feel that instinctual protectiveness that would have made me stop wavering about how I should raise her. This was grief's greatest exile: the separation I felt from my flesh and blood. The smallest tasks associated with her care flustered me. The prospect of arranging her gear for our outings— the network of bottles, diapers, and bibs—could send me into paroxysms of anxiety, as could the slightest outburst of her tears or discomfort. Any time I was confronted with the prospect of long, unbroken hours with my daughter, I ran— literally. I would drive to the beach, the same Weekapaug Cove where I had played high school tennis and now as a widower sat for hours listening to Ian McKellen narrate Homer's *Odyssey*, and I would retrace the steps of my high school training circuit. I would start my run at the point looking out toward Block Island, where on a summer day two years earlier in 2006 I had walked with Katherine's family the day before our wedding, hunting crabs and splashing barefoot on the shore, and then I would finish past the green-shingled Weekapaug Inn and the exquisite gray mansions along the coast, fronted by lush rose gardens that my father had pruned as a landscaper. Only afterward, because of the sheer exhaustion from a long run, would I be calm enough to return to my daughter and my family on the other side of town, a universe away from the solitude and peace I found only in exercise and isolation, two of the few aspects of life in the Underworld where I felt I could be in control.

One morning, just a month into my return to Rhode Island, I took the coastal road to Weekapaug to go running and stopped at a light, only to suddenly feel my car shake from an impact that sent me hurtling a few yards forward. I looked in the mirror and saw a drab SUV smothering my back view. I stormed out of the car and ran around to the driver, a young blond woman in shabby clothes who was clutching the wheel frantically. A policeman who had been parked in a nearby gas station drove over immediately to see what had happened.

"I'm so sorry," the girl cried. "I'm so sorry! Are you hurt?"

She was trembling as she spoke, as if to acknowledge her blame and hope that she hadn't caused anything serious. I guessed that she had been texting or making a call.

"Do you know what you just did!" I screamed, running over to the car. *"Do you know that my wife was just killed in a car accident!"*

By now the girl was in tears. The policeman made a beeline for me.

"You need to calm down," he said, putting himself between the girl's car and me and staring at me threateningly.

But I could not calm down. Everyday reality was difficult enough now that Katherine was gone, and to be suddenly struck from behind so soon after her accident shattered what little composure remained. Even I, a master disciple of the superego and sworn controller of the id, had to muster all my reserve to walk away quietly from the woman and return to my car.

I drove to the hospital and checked myself in to the emergency room, where the nurse, a friend of my sister Mary's, admitted me. Mary worked in the hospital in the records department and came down to see me right away.

"Are you okay?" she asked, with a gentle smile.

"She could've killed me," I spat out, still shaken. "This is how it's going to end for me, too."

She was not used to seeing me like this, a crumpled leaf. I had been the only one of my six siblings to leave town and make a life for myself elsewhere. But I had lost my stride and confidence, and a fender bender could make me quiver with fear. The man who always said the right things to the right people had just lost my shit in front of a cop and a teenage girl who ran a red light.

I DROVE UP ROUTE 1 from Westerly once a week to see Rosalind. I told nobody except my mother and sister Mary that I was seeking help, and I swore them to secrecy. I knew it was absurd to feel ashamed about speaking with a grief counselor under the circumstances, but it was all part of my inability to let go and loosen control, to admit to the world that my wife's death had brought me to my knees. People used to marvel: *Why, he's carrying on just like before, so brave, so strong!* But this was the problem. Katherine's death had asked me to switch gears, but I refused to decelerate. I actually shifted up, trying to barrel on ahead with life on a highway lane that her death had long since diverted.

Bard had generously offered me the opportunity to take a paid leave from teaching, yet I insisted on returning to the classroom. I threw myself back into the editing of my book. And I competed in tennis as though my life depended on it, playing my local league matches as if they were the Wimbledon final. I could have taken a step back and simplified things, spent months alone with Isabel in our Tivoli apartment, learned her rhythms and made her needs my own. Instead, I put all my energy into my career because I was frightened that, if I slowed down for one moment, I would lose what little endured of my identity. The same numbness that kept me from fully connecting with Isabel was also keeping me from fully absorbing Katherine's loss. And so I plowed ahead at all costs in a world of books and conference papers, academic articles over which I sweated blood, even though nobody read them, as though they were letters that I wrote to myself to prove that I was still living at my former address.

I don't know how much of this Rosalind saw because even with her I didn't completely let down my guard. I was as open as I was humanly capable of, which at the time was limited. I never lied—but I was selective in the truths I told. The shame of it all was that, as I played emotional chess with Rosalind, she was entirely open with me, exposing her own misgivings as a daughter and mother, the experiences that had made her into a healer. I could feel this fellow Rhode Islander loving me in the profound, impersonal way that her training had taught her. She had worked in hospices tending to the terminally ill. If I had ripped down the walls and told her some of the ugly, outrageous things that were festering inside me—how I resented my friends for the secure married lives they led while I slept alone at night, how my blood boiled when I thought of the driver who had struck Katherine's car, how ashamed I was by my dependence on my mother and sisters—she wouldn't have blinked. But she was wise and kind enough to take me on my own terms, even if she knew my confessions were only half the story.

It wasn't all gloom and doom, which made grief so difficult to fathom. A lot of my life went on just as before. I still enjoyed my meals and the occasional glass of wine and had even started to travel to visit friends. I still taught Dante and wrote learned articles and played tennis. Soon after the accident, I met a colleague and his wife for dinner at the Madalin, a hotel on the corner from my house in Tivoli. I was in the midst of the early, most savage phase of grief, when all I wanted to do was walk the frozen streets of my village and sleep curled up in a ball like Isabel—but then that night, suddenly, unexpectedly, the duck was delicious, the Sancerre luscious. The soft light in the dining room gave off a warm glow, enveloping happy couples and groups of friends at tables and bars, as all were laughing, drinking, eating, toasting one another and the holidays. The port wine reduction sauce on the glistening duck fat felt so good going down, it was as though I could taste what my former life had been, its balance of the sweet and the sour. The reprieve from my misery inspired generous thoughts: I told my friends that I would do all I could to keep Katherine's spirit alive, though I had no idea what this truly meant.

"That's incredible, Joe," they commented, eyes filled with admiration, before one of them described how a friend of hers had established a five-kilometer run in memory of a lost loved one.

The thought was well intentioned, but it deflated me. The 5K race—as though against fate itself—seemed a futile and insignificant gesture in the face of tragedy, making my own promises to keep Katherine a living presence sound just as naive. And yet I continued to savor my duck, the company of my friends, our conversation. All around us the atmosphere was soaked with the jokes and declarations of joyful people, some of whom had wept uncontrollably just days earlier at Katherine's memorial service. The world moved on, I knew this. I just didn't expect that part of me, too, would also move on, and so quickly after Katherine's death—that a delicious meal and delightful company could be just as appealing in the immediate aftermath of the accident as they were before. Grief was unrelenting but it was also uneven, its turbulent waters sometimes calm and relaxing.

And I still had my urges. Acting on them was out of the question. I wasn't going to have a fling, and had decided I would wait. For what, I wasn't sure, but my sense was that at some point I would transition—not quite as awful a word as "facticity" and "former life," but close—into a new relationship seamlessly and completely, without any of the awkward intermediaries like dating, misunderstandings, near misses, and total disasters. This romantic pipe dream was another element of my magical thinking.

There was someone I could not keep out of my thoughts—someone whom the friends I shared duck with had introduced to Katherine and me at a party just months earlier. This woman had undergone her own tragedy, the loss of a spouse and the birth of a child in extremis, and not long after Katherine died she sent me a friendly note of condolence. I kept her letter in a special place on my desk in Westerly and would turn to it from time to time, almost in prayer. It was a piece of salt-free bread that had somehow turned up on the table of my exiled city. The note symbolized my problem with Rosalind, my family, and my daughter in a nutshell: I just didn't want to change. I wanted my old life back. *My former life.* If not with Katherine, then with another woman who could restore what death had stolen. I could talk with Rosalind until I was blue in the face, tell her all my hopes and fears, doubts and dramas, but when it came down to it I was more interested in rebuilding my personal life than anything. Of course I missed the scent and touch and voice of a woman beside me, sometimes so much that it made me tremble. But what I missed most of all was being loved by a woman—being the center of another person's world, with all the trust, support, and companionship that come with this. I still loved Katherine, but I had lost her love for me, a love that had been my home. It was all so impossibly simple and yet inexpressible at the same time—"I'm sorry, Rosalind, everything you say about my needing to forgive myself and embrace my family's help and be proud of all the strides I've made with Isabel makes sense, but what I really need is a *girlfriend*. I mean, a wife. And while we're at it, I also need a mother to my daughter . . ." I couldn't say these things because they would have seemed what they actually were: desperate and unrealistic, at my early and raw stage of grief. Better that I held my tongue and heeded Rosalind's words that it was too soon for anything and everything.

Better, as Dante says in the canto after Ulysses, that this tongue of flame stops flickering.

Every night I went to sleep terrified of dreaming about Katherine. There was a sound in the room next to mine, a rhythmic breath as steady as the forward movement of time. My daughter was sleeping. She was alive. She had made it to the other side. My college president had called my plan to move back to Rhode Island harebrained, but he might have used Dante's words about Ulysses' shipwreck: it was a *folle volo*, mad journey. Neither love for his wife nor fondness for his son could keep Ulysses in Ithaca. But the breath of my daughter was keeping me tethered to the land of the living. I was yearning for the one thing that Dante's Ulysses had turned his back on: *dolcezza per mia figlia*, sweet devotion to my daughter.

Ulysses' words used to strike me for their rhetorical force and drama: he is a flickering tongue of flame hissing with lethal eloquence. But Katherine's death changed my understanding of him. Ulysses returned to Ithaca after a lifetime of adult wandering, and now I had returned to my hometown, the place where I was born and raised, after years of decidedly less-dramatic wandering. Yet, like Ulysses, when I took the sheets of childhood in my arms the scent made me sick. Sometimes you cannot go home again. Like the Greek hero, I had to digest Dante's most bitter lesson: the worst exile is internal, when you are cast forever from what had been your life—*com' altrui piacque*, as pleased another or fate decreed. The genius of Dante's Ulysses is that he shows how the most intense feeling of dislocation can occur in the most familiar of places. I returned to Westerly seeking a respite from my grief, a place where I could mourn Katherine in safety and peace. I found myself instead just as restless and anxious there as Ulysses was in Ithaca in *Inferno* 26. Like Ulysses, I learned that once exile becomes a state of mind, even your childhood home can seem as strange and unwelcoming as Calypso's cave.

Those first months in Westerly I would take Isabel to the coast and push her stroller along the shore. The ocean winds would snap and sting as I bundled her in a blanket and guided her along the same two-mile stretch that I had run while training for my high school tennis team. Weekapaug's grand, austere homes were always most beautiful in winter, when there were no crowds or traffic to distract your eye from the stark contrast between the gray shingles and the blue ocean. I saw myself in Isabel's jet-black hair and full lips, but I could not see her natural mother anywhere, except for her blue eyes. With each passing day those blue eyes were becoming slightly more like the brown color of mine, making me wonder what, if anything, of Katherine would be left in her. We would finish our walk at the very spot where I had listened to McKellen narrate Odysseus's journey. Wrapping the blanket tightly around Isabel, I would pick her up and look in the direction of Block Island, which you could make out on a clear day. If the wind wasn't too strong, I could hear Isabel's breath fall on my shoulders as I held her to keep her warm.

Katherine had gone to the other side, but she had left someone behind. My heart would race as I pondered this *vita nuova*—a life without Katherine—that I wanted no part of. Then I would feel Isabel's breath. It was more than time: it was life, hope.

Perhaps even a map out of the dark wood.

We were far from where we should have been, and I had never planned to share my childhood coastline with her so closely. But in those few moments that I held her, I understood that the rocks and houses and water were just things, places and spaces on a map like any other. They were no longer my home.

Home was my daughter's breath on my shoulder.

SOON AFTER RETURNING TO RHODE Island I received an invitation from the Westerly Dante Society, asking me to speak about my work on Italy and Italian culture, the two Italies of my southern Italian parents' violent immigrant world and the northern Italian cultural splendors that I had devoted my career to.

The Westerly Dante Society was founded in 1975 by second-generation Italian Americans whose parents and grandparents had fled the Old Country and its poverty for a better way of life in the United States. Men and women like my neighbor, Concetta McGuire née DeSantis, and my high school guidance counselor, Edward Gradilone, filled its ranks and carried on its mission: to celebrate the riches of Italian culture, including the genius the society was named after, Dante Alighieri.

I spoke in a converted bank in downtown Westerly to an audience of about fifty, most of whose parents or grandparents had been born in Italy. They were all thrilled to hear how my Calabrian upbringing had inspired me to become a professor of Italian, as they were to learn about the connection between their immigrant world and Italy's celebrated culture. I showed them a slide of a 1967 Chevy Impala, the *macchina* that my father mistakenly called a *carro* (cart) in his Calabrian dialect, to make it sound like the American *car*. He had purchased it the year I, his first American child, was born. Each audience member had his or her version of the Chevy Impala: the emblem of a family's transition to the new world. Almost all of us in the converted bank were linked by southern Italian blood.

"Joey, your family must be so proud," my best friend's grand-mother, an eighty-something matriarch of Calabrian descent, said to me after my talk. "To hear you speak about their background like this."

There I was, singing of my family's Calabrian roots while in reality I was recoiling from their Calabrian approach to child care.

"Thank you," I replied, hugging her. "I hope they are."

The motto of the Westerly Dante Society, an homage to the immigrant families who created our town, is from the canto of Ulysses: "You were not made to live as brutes, / but to follow virtue and knowledge." These honeyed words, which had inspired Ulysses' crew to abandon their families and follow his dream to the death, are preceded by a phrase:

Considerate la vostra semenza.

The phrase can be translated as "remember your origins," but the literal meaning—especially for a father trying desperately to connect to his daughter amid the shipwreck of grief—hit home much harder:

Consider your seed.

CHAPTER 3

Love–40

There's a dirty secret that everyone who has lost a loved one knows but will never dare share. If they did, it would sound wrong and stilted, repulsive even. Faced with sudden death, you slip into a state that, however awful, heightens your sensations and feelings. Everything becomes more intense. You lose all sense of proportion, just like a child who tries to draw a face and focuses all his attention on the nose, distorting the other features.

But that's not the dirty secret.

The thing you can't tell people is that grief is electric. Your life goes from its routines, its minor skirmishes and major battles, to total war. Suddenly everything matters as death infuses its awful gravity. Grief may be the most difficult thing you will ever go through, but its intensity carries a charge, no matter how painful. I knew that Katherine's death, and its connection with Isabel's birth, was the most momentous thing that had ever happened to me, and that it would divide my life into two halves, before and after. I also understood that how I handled her death would define me forever. It was all part of the loneliness that came with grief: the illusion that it was somehow all a personal challenge. Grief tends to breed such mania. When someone you love dies, the air around you becomes electric.

Nobody knew this better than the man who taught Dante how to write poetry: Guido Cavalcanti. Born in 1255 or 1256 to one of Florence's wealthiest families, Guido had it all. Handsome and brilliant, he was the finest lyric poet of his generation—so fine, in fact, that he became the unofficial leader of an entire movement: the *Dolce Stil Novo* that pushed the verbose Francesca into the arms of the silent Paolo.

In Guido's hands, the Sweet New Style became a surgeon's scalpel that probed a single question: what is love?

For Guido, it was a physical phenomenon that electrified the air, as we read in one of his most celebrated poems:

Who is she coming, watched by all
As she walks with Love beside her
And makes the air tremble with clarity,
Reducing men to sighs without words?

Guido's lady imposes herself like quiet lightning, her beauty confounding all who try to apprehend her. In 1293, the twenty-eight-year-old Dante dedicated the *Vita Nuova* to Guido, calling him his *primo amico*, best friend. For the young Dante, Guido's poetry offered a model of how to fall in love and write about the female body. For me, a year into my grief over Katherine's death, Guido's poetry expressed the confusing situation I found myself in. I was still in love with Katherine, but she was no more. I could continue to love her in spirit—indeed, this was a feeling that I imagined I could carry with me to the grave. But I could no longer love her body. The earthly connection that had joined us was forever severed. This was exactly where Dante found himself in the *Vita Nuova*, when Beatrice died young and tragically—except that Dante had never loved Beatrice's body. Her spirit was all that he had ever known and desired—that and the sight of her, once when he was nine and then again when he was eighteen. Guido, on the other hand, loved his women for their bodies, and he knew even better than Dante how physical love—both in its absence and its presence—can make the air electric.

LESS THAN A WEEK AFTER Katherine's death, I began to keep a journal, arranging each of my entries under different headings. Some were literary, in a self-pitying way (*A Season in Hell*). Others just as bookish but with a self-help twist (*Only Connect*). Some were hokey (*Miracle Baby*). None felt like writing. They were more silent cries than articulate statements, words that I wrote down to prove that I still functioned. I hadn't forgotten the rules of syntax and grammar, and the sentences in my journal all made sense. Sometimes my attention to form bothered me: *If I really loved Katherine*, I wondered, *wouldn't I be incapacitated?* After the neurosurgeon announced that he had been unable to save Katherine, I walked into the waiting room and in an instant my loved ones there knew. I was crying, they were crying, but I was still in one piece. My Calabrian ancestors used to wail and keen when someone they loved died, some even *sbalangavano la casa*, "ripped the house to pieces." I threw nothing, nor did I so much as groan. Why hadn't I been able to express my anguish? In Homer's *Iliad*, the Trojan King Priam rolls in the dust and spreads cow dung on his beard when he learns of his son Hector's death. I was just as obliterated, and yet there I was, giving hugs and handshakes.

I began my journal a few days later with thoughts of an East German city I had visited only once, over twenty years before, and for less than two hours.

In 1989, after graduating from college, I moved to Paris, and within months of my time there I began to see European history unfold before my eyes. After my late shift as a bartender off the Champs-Élysées, I would pick up *Le Monde* or *Libération* and bring it with me to a park near my apartment. In the middle of the night and under a streetlight, I sat and read of the Berlin Wall tumbling down, about Václav Havel leaving prison to become president of Czechoslovakia, Gorbachev with his extravagant birthmark shaking the Cold War to its core. I wanted to see it all firsthand.

So in May of that year a friend and I took a train from Paris to Prague, passing through Berlin. When we arrived at the Czech border, the guard inspecting our passports began to point at them. Neither of us understood a word of Czech, but we gathered that something was wrong.

"*Vizum. Vizum*," the guard said, drilling his finger against our passports. He was a massive blond bear with a baby face and a machine gun, and he was not smiling.

"*Vizum!*" he kept repeating, and by now we realized that we had neglected to secure the necessary visa. In a mix of English, French (which I spoke decently), and German (which I knew a few words of), I tried to explain that in the new Czechoslovakia, after the fall of the Berlin Wall, no visa was required—or so I had thought, or so I had read. He quickly had enough of us, two would-be American bohemians (I in my ponytail, my friend with his earring stud), and motioned for us to follow him down the long rusted corridor of the Iron Curtain train, where he conferred with other brawny and sour blond men in uniform. Within ten minutes, we were escorted off the train in East Germany, in Dresden, with instructions to take the first train back to Berlin for our visas.

I had read of Dresden in Kurt Vonnegut's *Slaughterhouse-Five*: Florence-on-the-Elbe, a magnificent collection of spires that the Allies bombed nonstop in 1945. Hundreds of British and American planes dropped thousands of tons of bombs on the city center, reducing it to charred rubble. Payback for the London air raids. At least twenty-five thousand Dresdeners died, mostly women and children.

My friend and I arrived in Dresden wracked by a hunger like I had never known before, because there was no end to it in sight. We had eaten the last of our travel biscuits and drank the last of our bottled water hours ago. We left the station hoping to find someplace that took U.S. credit cards, but it was five a.m., and this was East Germany. I came upon a large gloomy woman selling apples and sausages. The smell was torture. My friend watched with eyes wide as I made a beeline for her.

"*Apfel. Würstel,*" I said, pointing to the juicy red fruit and sausage.

She spat out the price without looking up. I opened my wallet. "*Keine ostdeutschen Mark,*" I said, "No East German marks."

She sized me up. I apparently didn't look like the homeless, vagrants, junkies, and other lost souls who showed up asking for free food. She registered the fear written on my face. But she didn't budge.

"*Apfel! Würstel!*" I insisted, pointing at the food.

My friend tried to pry me away. "Let's go, man," he said, pulling on my jacket.

I wouldn't be stopped. I thought of stealing the food, but I held back. Maybe this is why the woman finally relented. Perhaps she sensed that I wasn't the kind of person to do something illegal, that this was a one-off moment of true desperation. With a blank face, and without a hint of kindness or condescension, she handed over the apples and sausage.

After my friend and I wolfed them down, he gave me a look. We had been close for years and he thought he knew me. But he had just seen me beg. He seemed to be processing what he had just witnessed and what it said about me. I would do anything to get that apple and sausage, he realized, even if it got ugly. From beneath the surface of our easy, privileged lives, he had seen something animal in me, the naked hunger to survive, and it spooked him.

When I began my journal after Katherine's death, the first words I wrote were: *Call me Dresden.*

Among the entries were a series of lists—simple to-dos meant to keep me busy, when all I wanted was to walk around my neighborhood or wander through the aisles of Barnes & Noble. I would remind myself to do things like "wash and shave" and "go to the post office," then once I had completed the task I would write "done" in bold beside it. From the beginning, I was treating death—sudden death—as a challenge that I vowed I would survive. Not once, in that entire grieving time, did I fail to get out of bed, take care of daily business.

And yet I was absent from the person and the task that mattered most, Isabel and fatherhood. I lied to myself that I was spending as much time with Isabel as my work and commuting schedule allowed. In truth, I had rushed back to the classroom less than two months after Katherine died, just as I had thrown myself back into my scholarship while in the midst of my most intense grief. My family could not understand why I would spend hours on my academic research when I wasn't teaching (which for them meant not working, which in turn meant I should be with Isabel). In their defense, even when I wasn't teaching and writing, the thought of my next conference paper, academic article, or administrative move distracted me. And when I wasn't doing academic work, I was on the tennis court or at the beach, running and sweating to the point of exhaustion. I had always been rigidly routinized; grief had ratcheted this up to obsessiveness. I needed to be back at work, away on the tennis court, anywhere but around my family, because they reminded me of the shame I felt in passing Isabel over to them.

Worse still, I was finding I had little in common with the people I loved most, my mom and siblings. There was no *New York Times* in their houses, few if any books, no desire to talk about world events—all the things that had become part of my life ever since leaving Rhode Island at eighteen. I had stepped into a time machine, back into a childhood world where everyone—though now older and thicker—still had the same interests and predilections as when I had left. But I had changed, and the new me had found no comfort in what I thought would be my ultimate sanctum, the little white house with the green shutters and sloping backyard on Batterson Avenue in Westerly.

So I took refuge in the tennis court and the classroom, where I could maintain at least the outward appearance of living a normal life. I have always been the kind of person who keeps up appearances—as my grief counselor, Rosalind, was learning. Katherine's accident had reinforced my conviction that the world was a place of chaos and disorder, so I was determined to control what little of my life I could. I monitored my daily tasks like a trader managing his portfolio of stocks. I would do anything to show that I was still standing, that death had failed to defeat me. Inside I was King Priam smearing his skin with shit and rolling in the dust, an exploded shell of a human being struggling with a monumental loss. Nobody saw this. The image of sanity I projected to the world was both a mask and a barrier—the cast-iron casing that wouldn't allow even those who loved me most a peek inside at the mess of raw grief.

I had lost the woman I loved. I was now condemned, like Paolo and Francesca, to loving a woman without a body. Because in truth, this was one of my deepest connections to Katherine: her body, our bodies. We talked of cultural things, we visited museums together. But what had drawn me to her were not her views on Impressionist painting or Existentialist philosophy. With her I felt I could be the person I had grown up as, a Luzzi with the soft *z*. Katherine and I shared the same values, and she moved gracefully through life with none of the self-consciousness and self-denial that had propelled me along my entire life. I lived and taught and worked in a world of ideas; Katherine brought me down to earth. Our love was earthly.

In death's cruel irony, as I pined for her lost beautiful body, I became obsessed with taking care of my own body. This can happen when you fall into the Underworld. Surrounded by so many disembodied memories and weightless souls you become desperate for *cose salde*, solid things.

As the weeks after her death stretched into months, I continued to go on long walks, long runs, anything to free myself from the letters I had to answer, phone calls I had to return. I documented everything in my Dresden journal, especially the physical tasks that I completed and honored with a checkmark beside them. I knew I had to be physically strong to survive Katherine's death, and I had always relished exercise and sports. One sport above all—my first and oldest love.

MY HOMETOWN WESTERLY IS A short drive to the jewel of Rhode Island, Newport. I visited there many times as a child on school trips to the mansions on Bellevue Avenue, where I stood in awe of the marble balustrades of Rosecliff and the oceanic lawns of the Breakers. In my college years, Newport became synonymous with hedonism and bacchanals—my best friend studied at Salve Regina, the site of many a brain cell–destroying road trip. But never, as a child or adult, had I set foot on the grass of one of the city's most imposing landmarks, the Tennis Hall of Fame, a building I'd worshiped from afar since I was a boy. The site that houses the Hall, the Newport Casino, was originally built as a resort for the wealthy in 1880. When Newport's status as America's country club waned after the Great Depression, the Casino fell on hard times and was nearly demolished to become a shopping mall in what is today a bulging retail strip. But if you look closely enough at the Hall and the surrounding streets, you can still feel old Newport. The freshly painted colonial town houses on Spring Street recall the city's eighteenth-century colonial architecture, and the winding drive along Ocean Avenue seems made for the elegant carriages and shining chrome motorcars of America's Gilded Age and Roaring Twenties.

Newport and its Hall represented a genteel New England that was off-limits to me, an Italian American boy from an immigrant family. Here was the temple of the sport I loved, but it was anchored in a WASP tradition whose white flannels would only be stained red by my family's oily tomato sauces.

Tennis entered my life by chance. At Southern Methodist University, my older brother Angelo roomed with a nationally ranked junior, Woody Blocher, son of a DuPont executive and later the coach of U.S. Open quarterfinalist Tim Wilkinson. A quick athletic study, Angelo picked up the game from Blocher and his golden circle. He took me out one day to the asphalt courts of Tower Street School in Westerly when I was ten. He played with a Wilson T–2000, a barbaric trampoline of suspended steel and string that Jimmy Connors somehow wielded with otherworldly precision. My brother beat me 6–0 after firing an embarrassing number of aces up the tee. I burned with the desire for revenge; but I also felt something else stirring inside, a melting feeling that this game would always be a part of me.

I began to play nonstop, year-round. Even when it snowed, my best friend and I shoveled the sloping Tower Street court where my brother had beaten me at love, battling beside drifts and banks as tall as us. All the joys and sorrows of the tennis autodidact were mine: I never learned to punch a volley and couldn't drive a mid-court ball to save my life. But I had decent touch and the iron desire to win. If there were any poetic justice, I would have brought my Donnay Borg Pro with me to the junior prom instead of the green-eyed Anne Steele.

Expensive tennis lessons were out of the question for my family. I only had one my entire childhood, with a square-jawed pro whose flat forehand came at me so hard I thought it would break my wrist. Nor could I play indoors at our local Ocean Vista Racquet Club, in the hushed part of town along the coast with its weather-beaten shingles. For the vinyl-sided Luzzis, Ocean Vista was as distant as the Newport Casino.

Like many tennis-obsessed kids of my generation, my idol was Bjorn Borg, whom I copied down to his Donnay racket, colorful headbands, and habit of blowing into his hands to dry off the sweat. "He makes *five million* a year," I would tell my mother, as I sat mesmerized before one epic battle of Borg's after another with John McEnroe, a player I despised for everything he represented: a skidding slice to Borg's looping topspin, his visible self-torture to the Swede's stoic serenity, a lefty canti-levered serve to Borg's classic right-handed raised-arm delivery.

My early affair with tennis reached a fever pitch on July 4, 1980, when as a twelve-year-old boy I watched Borg and McEnroe play for the Wimbledon final. Portions of the match are easily found online, and compared to the viciously struck balls and space-age rackets of today, the white balls issuing from the tiny wood frames seem recorded in slow motion.

Extended rallies were rare, and many of the points ended in miss-hits, especially on McEnroe's leisurely backhand return and Borg's unorthodox forehand volley. But to focus on these errors is like standing before a Velázquez and noticing only the accumulated debris obscuring the once-vibrant colors. For in one breathtaking thirty-four-point tiebreaker in the fourth set, Borg and McEnroe took the game to a new level.

After the routine early sets, the play suddenly escalated in the tiebreak, as both players delivered one winner after another with the match and tennis history—Borg was going for his fifth consecutive title—on the line. The atmosphere on Centre Court (the main court at the Wimbledon Championship), always so intimate, became suffocating, as the tension from the match radiated into the audience. Time and again the umpire had to scold the crowd ("Quiet please!") while the players prepared to serve or recover from a tightly contested exchange. At 15-all, Borg pulled McEnroe wide into the ad court with a knifed backhand volley. In full sprint, McEnroe lifted the racket head on his forehand and guided a reply, with just enough flicker of topspin, down the line and past an incredulous Borg. The subtle modulation of wrist and infinitesimal timing distilled McEnroe's raw tennis genius to its essence. He would save five match points in the tiebreaker, Borg six set points. Finally, what had developed into a roar of athleticism ended with a whimper: serving at 16–17, Borg followed in his serve and dumped—anyone who plays will know there is no better word—a forehand volley into the net, the ball clunking off his strings far from the racket's sweet spot. Somehow, McEnroe had fought off all those match points to survive into the fifth set. Somehow, and this is the most unusual story of that unusual match, Borg would find the composure and resolve to play a flawless fifth set, which he won at 8–6 with a backhand passing shot past his lunging opponent. "That's it!" the normally reserved BBC announcer Dan Maskell shouted as Borg fell to his knees. "He's done it!" Game, set, match.

After Katherine died, every moment in my life felt like a tiebreaker—which also goes by the name "sudden death."

Moments after his glorious backhand, Borg was captured in an uncomfortable close-up by the television camera. He looked stunned. He and McEnroe hadn't just played unforgettable tennis; they had electrified the air. Less than two years later, at the age of twenty-six, he would walk away from tennis for good.

AT THE START OF THEIR Wimbledon final, Borg and McEnroe had passed through a doorway inscribed with these lines:

> If you can meet with Triumph and Disaster
> And treat those two impostors just the same

I wrote these words from Kipling's poem "If" in my Dresden journal days after Katherine's death. If I could just hold on, I told myself—"hold serve," as they say in tennis, win those crucial games when you control the serve—then maybe things would start to turn. There's a dilemma that every tennis

player faces when he's down love–40, that is, when your opponent has won the first three points against your serve and
needs just one more to take the game: Do you stop trying in a
game you're likely to lose and conserve energy for the next one?
Andre Agassi once went so far as to catch his opponent's serve
at love–40 and race off the court. He was booed intensely and
has never been allowed to forget his antic. But was he really so
foolish? After all, he won the match. And would anyone dare
blame me, at this dreadful point, if I gave up on life and gave
in to grief?

Back in Westerly, and back to my obsession with tennis, I
began to think nonstop about Borg and McEnroe's epic match.
I returned to it partly because I had also returned to my childhood home and one of its most vivid memories: sitting on the
red shag carpet in our upstairs living room on the Fourth of
July in 1980, glued to the television as Borg and McEnroe bat-
tled it out on Centre Court. In coming back to Westerly, I was
circling back to this match and the magical spell it had always
held over me—a spell that I now believed would help me do
battle with grief, a formidable opponent that I began to think of
as an enemy staring across the net at me. Grief was an electric
state—and the most electric state I had known growing up in
Westerly was that twenty-minute tiebreak at Wimbledon, when
the balls seemed to move through statically charged air. *If you
can meet with Triumph and Disaster / And treat those two impostors
just the same*, Kipling's lines went. In the pristine real estate of
that long-ago match on Centre Court, I found a capsule of the

mighty struggle against sudden death that my life had fallen into.

Four thousand miles away from Kipling's lines inscribed at Centre Court, a plaque in the Ocean Vista Racquet Club locker room commemorates Borg and McEnroe's historic Wimbledon match. "Borg wins torrid final" in bold print stands above a photo of Borg on his knees, raising his black and orange Donnay racket with the long leather handle, beside an image of McEnroe sprawled on the ground after an exchange from their tiebreaker.

Beneath the bold print announcing Borg's victory lies a notice in much smaller font in the paper's lower-priced real estate for niche sports. The little headline reads: "Newman, Villeneuve win Lime Rock features; rookie driver killed." Growing up, I had passed that framed clipping many times without a thought on my way to the courts. But now the rookie driver's death became inseparable from the Wimbledon headline towering above it. The defining moment of my life had become the death by car of someone who, like the driver, would remain anonymous to the world.

Within a year after Katherine's death, and by the time my Rhode Island exile had become a way of life, the Ocean Vista Racquet Club became my refuge. I started playing there soon after arriving in Westerly as part of my plan to infuse my *vita nuova* in Rhode Island with the lifelong passions that connected my childhood and adulthood. On my first visit, I signed up for a half-hour lesson; the hitting pro showed up ten minutes late. He lumbered about the court and sprayed forehands with a 1930s Continental grip. After twenty mirthless minutes, he moved on to the next assignment. A week later I received a bill for the full lesson, with no discount for the pro's lateness. I had expected more from the club than an invoice, especially since I was a prospective member. But their message was clear: we're here if you want to do business with us, but let's not pretend it's anything more than that.

Here was my Westerly life in a nutshell. The person I had become elsewhere didn't translate into the local dialect. In this community of tight-knit families and friendships stretching back to grammar school, you needed to check your credentials at the door and be a team player. I was unwilling to do so. In my mad climb for honors I believed, somewhere deep within, that I was better than all these locals who had remained behind in their metaphysical village, while I went out and scaled the ivory tower. It was an ugly, vain, misguided sentiment that, on a conscious level, embarrassed me; but unconsciously it fueled my every step. In Westerly I saw only my family, socialized with nobody outside of the tennis court. My cousins, my doubles partners—they all would have let me in had I only allowed them. But I was too conscious of my doctorate, my scholarly bibliography, my fancy friends, to just relax and be a Westerly Luzzi. I was still running from the shame of opening my lunchbox in high school and hearing the kids laugh as the oil from my pepper-and-egg sandwich dripped onto my sleeve, its redolent odor a stark contrast to

---

their antiseptic—and, I imagined, all-American—peanut butter-and-jelly sandwiches.

One day at dusk that first summer in Rhode Island, I stood in the warm sun of the Ocean Vista tennis courts and felt the moist air on my skin. Several months had passed since the funeral, and I was still standing. But in order to do so I had hurtled back in time to high school, when life was a series of long training runs on the beach, preparing for my tennis matches. The only order I now found in life was inside the lines of Ocean Vista's green clay courts, a place of perfect symmetry where you could check the ball mark to see if a closely contested shot had landed in or out. The situation was preposterous for someone like me, who had negotiated his way out of Dresden without a visa or a deutsche mark. But then again, I was not in my right mind. The air was electric, and even I, a hyper-controller, could not orchestrate the currents.

Meanwhile, I watched the Borg-McEnroe tiebreaker obsessively. While Isabel slept in the room beside me either at my mom's or, very rarely, in her room at my rented apartment in Westerly, I cued up the grainy video and paused to catch the athletes' expressions, usually while sitting on that same red shag carpet in the living room where I had watched the match live as a twelve-year-old. The two players were locked in struggle, just as I was, and I longed to channel McEnroe's intuition and creativity, Borg's calm and strength. Their antithetical styles of play revealed two different models of grieving, one all Dionysian fury, the other a cool Apollonian mask.

I often paused the DVD at 5–6 in the tiebreaker, with McEnroe down match point and about to deliver his second serve. Anyone who plays tennis understands the particular challenge of a second serve: it's a thankless task. The second serve is rarely a winner and functions primarily to keep the point going for the server. It's usually noticed only when you mess up and double fault, point to the enemy. There's a saying, "you're only as good as your second serve," and when the pressure is on even the mighty blink: up 5–2 in the fourth-set tiebreaker of his magnificent 2008 Wimbledon final against Roger Federer, Rafael Nadal was two points from victory when he double-faulted to let Federer back into the match on a second serve so weak (83 miles per hour) that you could almost read the label on the ball midflight. The French call this *avoir le petit bras,* "to have the shrunken arm"; in English we say choking.

Down 5–6 in the tiebreak, McEnroe leaned back, propelled forward, and delivered his second serve. It was in play and pulled Borg wide enough so that McEnroe could launch forward and clip the return for a winning volley. Match point saved.

Aside from the classroom and the library, the tennis court was the lone space where I could escape my family and free myself from the burden of their expectations as to how I should be raising Isabel. "Have you ever taken her for more than *four hours* straight, without our help?" a sister once asked me. Isabel herself never came with me to the courts, which were one of a series of places where I would go to mourn Katherine's loss, sometimes directly and sometimes indirectly. My hunger for solitude was insatiable: the apartment across town from my mom's house in Westerly, the Tivoli loft I now occupied alone, my side of the net on the Har-Tru clay of Ocean Vista—they were all stations of grief's cross, where I could work or sweat or struggle to rid myself of the furious psychic energy that I felt might otherwise devour me.

Months after Katherine's death, I was coming to terms with the most difficult part of her loss, which was not the initial shock and tailspin of grief. It was the new grim reality that came with it. The work of having to adjust to a new life, a *vita nuova* I wanted no part of as I settled into my Rhode Island routine.

Each Thursday, I would drive to Westerly from Bard after my week's teaching was over, pulling into my mother's driveway around suppertime, just as she was spooning Lipton soup or Velveeta macaroni and cheese into my daughter's mouth, opened trustingly like a baby robin's about to receive a worm from its mother. Isabel's brown eyes—they had in fact changed color as she grew—lit up when she saw me, the man who was the other anchor of her life outside of her *nonna* and who would disappear for a couple of days, always to return. After I played with her on the red shag carpet in the living room, rolling a ball between us or sounding out the words in one of the many Italian picture books I bought for her, my mother would put Isabel to bed and I would drive to my rented apartment for a few hours of writing and reading before returning to my mom's, to sleep across the hall from my daughter.

The next morning, on Friday, we would go together to the aquarium. We would start at the tropical fish and make our way toward the shark tank. Isabel would put her face within inches of its razorlike teeth as it circled listlessly around the seals and turtles. Like the little fish protected from the sharks, we were tucked inside a matronly Luzzi bubble, buffered against the wild open sea and its scary creatures. Isabel had been violently wrested from a mother's womb, and now we had landed back inside Yolanda Luzzi's cloistered world, whose impregnable barriers enabled me to function while the grief ate away at me.

I would stare at our reflection in the fish tanks and see a father and his daughter stare back—the image I desperately yearned for but could not seem to make last. By noon, after we had visited the usual corridors of tanks, I would drive us back to my mom's and drop her off while I went to edit my proofs across town, sealing myself for a few hours in a solitary room and poring over books and papers in silence—the closest I would come to true prayer.

These visits to the aquarium stretched from Isabel's infancy into her toddler years as a kind of sacred ritual that gave me hope of our becoming a true father-daughter team. They were also a brutal index of my years of exile. At first I would wheel her down the dark corridors of tanks in her stroller. But by the later years of our Rhode Island time—when Isabel was old enough to walk with me up the bleachers of the auditorium—I often took her to the dolphin show. She would squirm, still too young to follow the balletic lines in the air of the magnificent streamlined cetaceans and much happier by the homely puffer fish, whose flaps she would trace with her finger on the glass enclosure. As the dolphins soared, I would stare at her and wonder why I hadn't dropped everything, swept her in my arms and moved back to Bard to build a quiet life for just the two of us. That's the problem with grief: you're sick, but you don't have a fever or a sore throat, and your limbs work fine. Nobody can see the rubble and debris inside, your inner Dresden.

For those few hours every Friday morning, Isabel and I looked like a father and a daughter. Then the dolphin show ended, and it was time for lunch and the usual tussles about no French fries and just one cookie.

My daughter, from the first, had the most lawyerly of dispositions. Anything, from the apportioning of desserts to the fit of her car seat, could inspire an impassioned plea that would expose the slightest inconsistencies in my parenting. She would wolf down a Chicken McNugget but reject out of hand a home-cooked chicken tender of infinitely freer range and choicer meat, by pointing to a fleck of black pepper I had let disastrously slip into the breadcrumb shell. And she would shrug off blankets of the finest wool if they weren't plastered with whatever toy design was capturing her interest at that particular time—an interest she would then eventually reject as completely déclassé when she moved on to her next enthusiasm, as Zhu Zhu Pets gave way to Thomas the Tank Engine who then ceded pride of place to the franchising genius of team Star Wars. My daughter, I was discovering, was no different from dear old dad in her devotion to unshakeable habit and routine, and I could sense that she was just as dependent as I was on these Friday visits to the dolphins. She was learning as much about me as I was about her, as she came to know how far she could push for that cookie or soda before giving up, and how close by I would stand, her hand in mine, as the shark ominously turned the corner and floated, dead-eyed and frowning, in her direction. Here we were, finally and rarely alone, in fleeting stabs at togetherness that we would roll out and then pack back up every Friday, as though parenthood were some kind of portable stroller.

As we drove back to Westerly from the aquarium, I would look into the rearview mirror and admire Isabel's shock of curly black hair and think of the thousand things I wanted to tell her about her mom. I wanted to describe the way that Katherine sprinkled salt on her food, making Florence's unsalted bread a stranger to her tongue. I thought of telling her how Katherine's lithe body was perfectly proportioned but strangely not made for running, as if her step was too light for the pounding of limbs required by sprinting and jogging. I would have liked to joke with Isabel about how her mom, even after years of spending time with me in Italy and trying to learn the language on her own, still pronounced Paradiso as *Para-dee-zee-oh*, part of her curious linguistic habit of adding extra vowels to the language, as if to make it sound even more Italian than it already was. As the inlets passed by our window, I wished above all to tell Isabel how sorry I was that these soul-defining imprints of Katherine were fading away into a formless gray elegy as I sunk deeper into the Underworld of ghosts and memories. And then Isabel would unexpectedly meet my gaze in the mirror, her hazel-brown eyes alert and open to the world. There was nothing angelic or ethereal in my daughter's eyes, nothing but the occasional flash of Katherine's look, giving me a final physical link to the woman no longer sitting beside me.

AND YET I WAS STILL in love with this woman who had left my side. Katherine's ghost seemed more vivid and present than the living, breathing women I would meet from time to time. Guido Cavalcanti once wrote a poem about falling so deeply in love with his lady that the poet himself was destroyed, leaving only his hands and writing instruments to speak:

We are the sad, bewildered quills,
The little scissors and the suffering penknife,
Who have written in sorrow
Those words you have heard.

When Beatrice died in the *Vita Nuova*, the young Dante was just as distraught as the ruined narrator of Guido's poem. All love is physical, Guido tried to teach Dante—there is no loving somebody without a body. At first, Dante accepted the wisdom of Guido's words and tried to find new love with the *donna gentile*, the lovely lady in the window who held the promise of erotic love. But by the end of the *Vita Nuova*, he understood that there was more to love than beautiful bodies and the air they leave trembling in their wake—a realization that would drive him away from Guido.

Guido's politics were just as radical as his poetry. He was a member of a violent faction that took part in assaults on Ghibelline families in 1300. In his capacity as prior, a leading official in Florence, Dante actually signed the edict banishing Guido from the city for his attacks. He was sentenced to exile in malarial Sarzana, where he fell seriously ill. Recalled to Florence, Guido died only months later, in June 1300. In *Inferno*, Dante meets Guido's father in hell, where he burns for the same Epicurean sin ("those who make the soul die with the body") associated with his son Guido. Technically speaking, Guido cannot be in hell yet because his actual death took place two months after the fictional date of *The Divine Comedy*, April 1300. But Guido's ghost haunts Dante by proxy in Inferno, through the ravaged and mournful figure of Guido's damned father.

Even before their political falling-out, Dante had become skeptical of Guido. Because, in truth, Guido was more a poet of death than of love. Everything that Guido wrote about, from gorgeous ladies who reduced men to stupor to quills forced to speak on behalf of a lovesick narrator, revealed how passion destroyed all in its path. As I grieved over Katherine's lost love, I understood all too well how the feelings of longing and unrequited desire can bring you to your knees. But I also was starting to understand, as no doubt Dante did as well, that there is more to love than an earthly bond—even when that bond was as powerful as mine with Katherine.

I first encountered death in my twenties, when my father, Pasquale Luzzi, passed away. I struggled for months afterward, unable to find the time or the space to mourn him. I was in graduate school and studying intensely for my doctorate, which gave me all the workload—and all the excuses—I needed to avoid confronting his loss. Then, the summer after he died, I took a job in Brittany, France, at an American art school, where my few duties left me a lot of free time to face his death in a quiet, beautiful setting. It was a long and lonely summer, but the work of mourning was necessary and, in its painful way, fulfilling.

During that summer I flew to San Francisco for a friend's wedding. On the way back, I had a layover at JFK airport in New York and called home, desperate to hear my family's voices. My only true companions that summer had been memories of my father and the lush paths outside of the Breton village of Pont-Aven, where I went on endless walks and runs, taking care to avoid the bales of hay bundled in barbed wire throughout the countryside. After speaking with my family, I went to TCBY and bought a frozen yogurt. I felt anguished, alone, buried in the loss of a man I had worshiped but barely known. I was walking down the long linoleum corridor of the ugly airport terminal, bracing myself for the return flight and more penance in the fields of Brittany, when suddenly my heart surged into my throat. My eyes blurred over, and I felt a sound, a silent sound—a chorus of music that I could somehow hear and see. I had never before and have never since experienced anything remotely similar, including after Katherine's death. I don't know who sent it—my dad, my maker, my imagination, my grief—but I do believe, as fervently now as I did twenty years ago, that it meant my father's spirit lived on, that our bond would never break, and that our love, that love itself, was eternal.

Even after a year of grieving for Katherine I had not yet gotten to the point where I could feel our love transcending the body and making it into spirit, as had happened with my dad. But, as Dante did with Beatrice, I held on to the hope and belief that this could and would happen.

I rejected—as Dante had, seven hundred years earlier— Guido's belief that the soul dies with the body.

ON SEPTEMBER 21, 2008, I made it through the "draw" (a first-round bye and then a semifinal match against someone twenty pounds overweight) of the Ocean Vista annual tennis tournament to face Kyle, a traveling salesman who lived not far from the Newport Hall of Fame, in the final. To say that Kyle and I were evenly matched would be like saying that two cloned sheep look alike to the naked eye. We had played hundreds of sets, and in the balance we may have won an equal amount of points. It was ever thus: our first set ended in a tiebreak. Yet our equality was hewn out of very different timbers: he was a compact, unassuming all-American Midwesterner, a Big Ten graduate who was happily married and the father of a baby boy. At Ocean Vista he was the guy next door everybody loved; I was the visitor, back in my hometown but a stranger to all. It was pretty clear that people would be rooting for the Buckeye.

I woke up the day of the final deliriously nervous. To calm myself, I went for a short run an hour before the afternoon match and worked out a game plan: Kyle was a superb base-liner, with short, well-timed strokes and good lateral movement. But he was uncomfortable in the transition game, moving from the baseline to the net to set up a volley or put away. So I decided I would feed him short angles and soft deep topspin balls, to take him out of his preferred strike zones and tire him out.

Then something completely unanticipated happened: my game plan actually worked. A few tight games that could have gone either way fell to me, and I found myself up a break early in the first set. This would normally be the time that the earth's gravity pulled Kyle even. But instead my lead widened, as Kyle sprayed the short balls he usually dined out on and bungled the soft topspin and angled drop shots I was feeding him. Before I knew it, I had taken the first set, 6–2.

I prepared myself for a reversion to the mean. But Kyle began to play even worse. I made few unforced errors, especially on my service returns, which were landing uncharacteristically deep and preventing Kyle from sliding into attack mode. Every tennis player in the world fears a meltdown when they are up comfortably, and I had the luxury of this concern with a 5–1 lead in the second set. *Stay focused. Stay in the moment. One point at a time.* I rehearsed all the clichés that a competitive athlete lives by in an effort to keep myself concentrated on the points at hand. Up 5–2, 40-love, I watched incredulously as Kyle dumped—just as Borg had to end his epic 1980 tiebreaker with McEnroe—one final ball into the net, which absorbed his harmless stroke and gave me the match.

After we shook hands, I slumped onto a wooden bench beside the court. I couldn't move as the elation flooded my clay-covered body. This was the first time I had been ecstatic, out-of-body happy all year. For the first time since Katherine died I was experiencing joy, the kind that floods your body. And in flooding my body it woke up my body. That part of me that was open to sharing love, physical contact, plea-sure, came to life on the green clay, after a year of slumber. The match terminated what had been a boot camp of endless hours on the tennis court, ostensibly devoted to improving my game and fitness. Hours that I could have spent playing with my daughter, teaching her Italian, even bouncing over-sized tennis balls with her against her miniaturized racket. But instead I had absented myself from Isabel and my family, sequestering myself inside those ordered, circumscribed lines of the tennis court, where I could vent all the pent-up rage, fear, and pain that my natural tendency to hide things and my desire to please prevented me from expressing in public. Some people turn to drink, some to porn, others to religion; I had chosen a clay rectangle by the sea.

My time in the Underworld was ending. It hadn't been a descent into hell, with burning sands and talk of lost redemption; it had been more like a walk through a suburban Detroit cemetery under a steady cold drizzle. Kyle drove away, and I sat on the court alone. There was nobody to share the victory with me, as was appropriate, because my time in the electric air of grief was the most intensely lonely, the most solitary I had ever known. All I could take care of that year was my body—not Isabel's. I may have looked healthy and played to win on the court, but I was also playing to distract myself from a situation I found unbearable. I had no business being in Westerly, not with the resources I had to raise Isabel on my own, and not with the choices I needed to make to ensure Isabel had the mall-free, junk-food-free upbringing that I would have preferred for her. But I was pining for my wife. I would never have told anyone this, but I had not gotten over losing her body, the warmth of her touch, my desire to fuse with her. Her spirit was not enough—Dante's Beatrice could not help me with this one. I was not ready for a love of Christian purity, which is why Guido's poetry, with its talk of beautiful women making the air tremble, made more sense to me than Dante's gorgeously sublimated verse about a perfect, pure Beatrice whom he had never touched. I was tired of worshiping Katherine's spirit. I wanted to touch a real body.

It was a glorious late September day the afternoon I defeated Kyle, and the light cast thick black shadows on the clay as it was descending into dusk. I could feel myself entering a new phase of grief, the time of mourning. It would be less terrifying than the previous months, but perhaps more difficult. I had felt largely anaesthetized in the year since Katherine died, concerned only with my own survival. Now I would have to join the living. Summer was ending. It was time to pack up my rackets and leave the soft clay.

Time to go where the air was no longer electric.

II

Mount Purgatory

Trattando l'ombre come cosa salda.
Treating shades as solid things.

II

CHAPTER 4

Astrid and Anja

My heart is racing.

It's November 2008, one month after my lone victory in the Underworld, beating Kyle in the Ocean Vista final. I'm lying naked in bed with the woman who had sent me the condolence card that I kept in a special place on my desk—the woman I dared not speak to Rosalind about. It's one year into the era of electric air that followed Katherine's death. The woman and I have matching PhDs, matching awful stories. To an outsider, nothing could be more deserving or healing than this embrace. But my heart is pushing against her breast, as though it's about to burst from my chest.

"What's the matter?" she says.

"It's not you," I say. "I just feel overwhelmed."

Before this night, Astrid and I talked for hours on the phone, detailing our lives with our late spouses and the lacerations that their sudden deaths had caused, followed by the miracles of our daughters' lives. Her daughter, Anja, was seven months old, born a year after the death of her father, Jorge, from a frozen egg of Astrid's that he had fertilized soon before succumbing to cancer. Isabel was eleven months old, born on the day of her mother's death. And now Astrid and Anja were visiting Isabel and me from Brooklyn, the four of us thrown together in a life-after-death experience.

Our first date had been in October. We had arranged to meet on the eleventh, just one day after Katherine's birthday and the anniversary of our meeting in Brooklyn in 2003. I couldn't bear the thought of meeting Astrid on that momentous day, October 10, and only exhaled after we had set the date for afterward. On Katherine's birthday, I fielded solemn messages from her family and mine, expressing their solidarity and commemorative sorrow. I ached too, but part of me was also bursting with anticipation. I was about to go and meet a woman for the first time in my second life.

The eleventh of October turned out to be a spectacular fall day. I put on my crispest blue blazer and pressed black dress pants, dressing up with thoughts of a woman's appraising eye for the first time in a year. As I shot my cuffs out from my jacket in front of the mirror, I thought of all the eternally mournful

Calabrian women I had known, how they would wear black tent-like dresses for years out of devotion to their late spouse. I too had donned an invisible cloak of black, but now I was putting on color again. I didn't tell my family about the rendezvous with Astrid the day after Katherine's birthday—the guilt was too overwhelming, so I made something up about going with a friend to see an exhibit at the Metropolitan Museum of Art. A friend once said to me that guilt is a mask for something else: the selfish desire to have our cake and eat it too, as we struggle to reconcile our true desire with our sense of obligation. I had laid out so many insulating layers between what I felt and how I acted that I didn't know whether I was ashamed or embarrassed by what I was doing. Maybe that was part of the thrill: the sense that desire was once again unsettling life's fixed routines.

Astrid walked into Bar Boulud on the Upper West Side, carrying Anja and smiling. Even in her casual jeans and loose-fitting shirt, she was resplendent. For months I had been orbiting my mother and sisters, a stranger to their world. Earlier that day I had left Isabel behind in their care so I could spend time with a woman from my intellectual village—someone who wouldn't blink at the mention of Defoe or Derrida, who could luxuriate in the ironies of Kafka and the long interior monologues of *Middlemarch*.

Uncharacteristically, I ordered a glass of wine with lunch and described to Astrid Isabel's finicky appetite. Astrid sang the praises of vitamin-infused porridge, and we both admired

Anja's chubby red cheeks. An old warm feeling was coming back, flooding my body. Desire, lust, the force that had propelled me as a man, that had savored Katherine's touch and taste. I held the Grüner Veltliner on my tongue, taking in Astrid's smell. A few hours later, we sat on a blanket in Central Park.

"I remember meeting Katherine," Astrid began.

She spoke in a thoughtful and respectful tone—more in solidarity with a fellow mother than with a fellow grieving spouse.

Astrid lost Jorge from cancer just months before Katherine died. Mutual friends of ours—the ones with whom I would share duck and Sancerre at the Madalin Hotel in Tivoli soon after Katherine's death—had told me some time before the accident about this couple who were madly in love and facing the unspeakable. Jorge, diagnosed with a terminal disease, had only a short time to live. I was paralyzed with sorrow. The thought of anyone, especially someone so young, having to suffer through the imminent death of a beloved partner seemed too cruel to bear. Soon after Jorge's death, a very pregnant Astrid appeared at a house party given by our mutual friends. After I arrived at the party with Katherine, who was also pregnant, the two mothers-to-be immediately found each other and, in gorgeous symmetry, talked of babies and childbirth.

As happily and entirely devoted to Katherine as I was, I could not help noticing the German woman's astonishing beauty and no-nonsense calm, as she carried herself with otherworldly poise, not revealing an ounce of self-pity or sorrow. We said a few polite words to one another, and I tried not to stare. I had been around long enough to know that the normal routines of life would soon enough smother any fleeting pulse of desire I felt for Astrid, someone I had no reason ever to see again. A passing image of her might rouse my thoughts; otherwise our lives would go their separate ways. But I carried a picture of her inside after we parted.

Later, Astrid would admit that she too had noticed me at that party and felt a passing attraction. But on our Central Park blanket, our first date as widow and widower, the light, happy chemistry was no place for confessions, as Anja sprawled between us and flashed me easy smiles. I picked her up, holding another woman's child in my arms while my own child was over a hundred miles away.

We discovered a common passion. Astrid, it turned out, had been in tennis's thrall for as long as I had.

"Do you hit with one hand or two on your backhand?" I asked.

"Two, of course."

"We have to play sometime."

When we said good-bye two hours later, I gave her an awkward peck on the lips that she accepted by looking me squarely in the eyes.

If only things could have stopped there. But of course they couldn't.

BEFORE DANTE TRANSFORMED HIM INTO deadbeat dad Ulysses, Homer's Odysseus journeys to the Underworld to meet the great warrior Achilles.

"[Achilles]," Odysseus says, "no man before has been more blessed than you, nor ever / will be. Before, when you were alive, we [Greeks] honored you / as we did the gods, and now in this place you have great authority / over the dead. Do not grieve, even in death."

You see, Odysseus is saying in effect, *you don't have it so bad here in the Underworld. You're the king of the dead. And even though people here don't have bodies, the air around you is electric.*

The great warrior, a man better known for his strength of body than his acuity of mind, gives an astonishing reply:

"O shining Odysseus, never try to console me for dying. / I would rather follow the plow as [slave] to another / man . . . than be a king over all the perished dead."

The souls in the Underworld aren't just dead to Achilles: they're "perished" dead. Dead twice over. A world without bodies means nothing to him. Achilles understands that however elevated you feel in the Underworld, it's no place to live. Eventually you need air, real air. And with air comes breath. With breath comes the rhythms of time, and with the rhythms of time come hope.

When Isabel and I stayed at my mom's, our rooms were across the hall from each other, two squat boxes of equal size that I had inhabited at different times growing up, depending on which sibling was getting married and moving out. Now I was back in the room I had slept in throughout high school, and it was arranged largely as I had left it, with the same sports trophies vying for space with the same family photographs. I kept my framed doctorate in this childhood room, the only substantive addition I had made to the décor since adolescence. Isabel, meanwhile, slept in a room bathed in pink and decorated with care by my sisters, who had filled the walls with images of playful animals and smiling relatives.

At night, I kept both of our doors open so I could hear her breathing.

In the profound loneliness of my grief, the only peace I found was in listening to my daughter's breath. I was utterly displaced, especially when I slept in the room I had grown up in, my childhood bed that had now become home to my adult sorrow. But there was her breath, its slow, soft rhythms as serene as the sapphire air of Purgatory. I stayed at my mom's and not my rented apartment in order to be able to hear Isabel breathe—and to show my family that I was trying as best I could to look after her.

E QUINDI USCIMMO A RIVEDER le stelle.

And then we emerged to see the stars again—these are Dante's last words in *Inferno*, as he draws in his final gasps of hell's electric air.

The moment he arrives in the next canticle, *Purgatorio*, the atmosphere changes:

The sweet color of oriental sapphire,
which filled the serene face
of the sky all the way to the horizon,
brought joy to my eyes once more,
as soon as I had left the dead air
that had saddened my eyes and heart.

These are among the most beautiful lines of poetry that Dante ever wrote. They aren't particularly profound or even thought-provoking: they are what they appear to be, six verses of pure musical rapture meant to conjure an atmosphere of relief. Their genius comes from their juxtaposition.

After the language of hell—all stony rhymes and hissing curses (*If I had verses harsh and grating enough / to describe this wretched hole . . .*)—Purgatory gives us words of sweet, oriental sapphire. Each penitent must purge himself of sin and ascend the top of Mount Purgatory en route to Paradiso. With these lines Dante does something far more powerful than tell us we are no longer in hell: he *shows* us by describing how the air has changed. It is soft, still, the air that humans breathe in the real world. The kind of air that Achilles would have relinquished his infernal crown for.

Early in *Purgatorio*, Dante writes:

Ma qui la morte poesì resurga . . .

But here let dead poetry rise . . .

Yes, the air up here is beautiful, Dante seems to be saying, *much more so than in the Underworld—but learning how to breathe again will be difficult.* Because the poetry of life is a lot different from the poetry of death. Because now you are back in the realm of climbing, purging bodies.

That's the key to moving from grief to mourning: saying good-bye to the electric air.

Before he could say good-bye to the Underworld, Dante had to answer a question that he had inherited from Guido: what is love?

In the *Vita Nuova*, when the ladies with the crazy hair frightened him, Dante believed that to love someone meant to be spellbound by her beauty. Then Beatrice died. She had served as his muse, the woman who had inspired him to *ragionar di amore*, speak of love. After her death, he learned that loving someone with a body is easy; loving someone without one is another story. A great story, it would turn out—but that would take time. Lots of time.

The answers would change, but for Dante the main question remained: what is love? In hell, Francesca da Rimini tried to give him the answer, but she talked too much while saying too little, and her eternal lover Paolo said not a word. Nobody in the Underworld could answer this question, not even the greatest writer in the history of Roman literature, Virgil, nor one of the greatest heroes in the history of ancient literature, Ulysses.

This just wasn't the kind of question anyone in hell could answer because to do so would require abandoning the prison of his own relentless self-regard.

What is love? The founder of modern psychoanalysis, Sigmund Freud—who spent a lifetime trying to figure out the kinds of psychological problems that landed you in Dante's hell—also had trouble answering the question. A friend of his, the French writer Romain Rolland, once told Freud that he believed in God because of the "oceanic feeling" that the sense of being alive gave him. Rolland felt the limitlessness of creation in his bones, which he took as a sign of the divine. He might have said: it's like falling in love and not being able to put it into words.

Freud countered that this so-called "oceanic feeling" was no more than the naked fear felt by a child who has been severed from his mother's womb and thrust into the world. For him the oceanic feeling was the psychological energy that arises as we develop consciousness and distinguish ourselves from the nonhuman world. He might have said: it's like falling in love and *trying* to put it into words. Freud was a lot like Guido Cavalcanti—he thought that you could answer the question "what is love?" with scientific analysis. Freud, like Guido, made it a question for the mind, not the heart.

Freud believed that when you lose your beloved, you need to spend lots of time in the Underworld with her ghost, slowly letting her lose her body and fade into pure memory. Mourning can only end when you have detached your passion and physical desire from your beloved. Freud uses an ugly term for passionate love: *libido.* Only after detaching your libido, he wrote, can you move forward and fall in love again. Again, he slaps an ugly description onto the process: *reattach your libido to a new object of desire.* According to Freud, that is how you get over your beloved's death.

It's a shame that Freud and Guido Cavalcanti never met. They would have had a lot to talk about.

When Dante redefined his notion of love in Purgatory's sapphire air, he did so in a poetic language that Guido and Freud would never have understood.

THE FIRST NIGHT ASTRID AND I spent together, my heart raced; hers beat evenly.

The youngest daughter of two schoolteachers, she had been taught from a young age to feel good about herself, her abilities, and her prospects. We both came from European families, though the similarity stopped there. My childhood was steeped in fearful and superstitious Calabrian history. Our household was a loving but chaotic mess. Even the shortest of trips to the supermarket for milk or the drugstore for aspirin were accompanied by my mother's religious exhortation, "*A Madonna ti guardasse*"—"May the Virgin Mary keep watch over you." The slightest of compliments, for a growing baby or promotion at work, was regarded by my family with dread, fearful that a jealous God would rain down misfortune as a corrective to human hubris. And my mother would counter the most benign of daydreams and wishes—a raise in salary, a retiled bathroom—with a catchall phrase reminding you not to take anything temporal and ephemeral too seriously in this harsh world: "*Stissima buoni, figlio mio, stissima buoni,*" she would say

("May our health keep, my son, may our health keep"), the accumulated centuries of Calabrian hardship and sorrow glistening in her brown eyes.

In terrific contrast, Astrid grew up in a steady household. My father would fall asleep in a haze of cigarette smoke and wine, his face contorted as if mid-nightmare after a sixteen-hour work day; Astrid's father would doze off in his study grading math exams and listening to a Haydn quartet or Handel aria, some piece of the classical music that accompanied most of his waking moments. My mother regarded physical labor as a necessity for the world's poor, and so would insist on being driven even the shortest of distances as a matter of pride; Astrid's mom was, to quote Astrid, *sportlich*, a sporty tennis enthusiast who was always running errands on her old-fashioned bicycle. Most tellingly, Astrid was encouraged to follow her interests and passions even when they led her away from her home country and hometown. Meanwhile, I was the only one of six siblings to move outside of a ten-minute radius from the house I had been raised in.

These dueling Calabrian and German childhoods played out in our daughters. My mom always referred to Isabel as *poverella*, "poor little one," as though she were a fragile thing requiring comprehensive maternal care to protect her from fate or happenstance. Astrid knew that kids were resilient, that they would bend but not break. So she explored the world with Anja in her backpack, the two of them flying from one continent and adventure to the next.

Isabel, meanwhile, stayed behind in Rhode Island to be cared for by my family in the only way we understood: according to routine. This meant going to bed in the same place at the same hour after having eaten the same foods. Isabel had to be protected from the promiscuity of germs, the delays of airplane security, and the clanging noises of hotels. While I fancied myself a modern man, I accepted that my daughter be raised along old-world Calabrian codes, letting the women do the heavy lifting, keeping my little weakling—or so I imagined her—away from the perils of life outside the hearth.

I didn't dare tell Rosalind that I had started thinking of Astrid again soon after Katherine's death. I kept quiet because I thought of Astrid not as a fellow sufferer in untimely death and instant parenthood, but because I wanted her as deeply as I did the first time I laid eyes on her. When I first saw her, the sensation was just a ripple of turbulence that was easily and quickly absorbed by the placid lake of marital fidelity. But, months into my widowerhood, it wasn't Astrid's body I desired as much as her—it sounded preposterous, but there was no other way to say it—*life*. I wanted to know what she was thinking and feeling as she faced her future after losing the person she was supposed to have shared it with, what her young daughter meant to her in the black hole of grief. The effortless gravitational pull of attraction that first put her in my orbit seemed incomparably simpler than my reaching out to grasp Astrid's thoughts and dreams.

Poor Astrid: she was about to encounter a man, as Dante would say, who insisted on treating shades as solid things.

AT THE BOTTOM OF MOUNT Purgatory, Dante hears singing
that arrests him in his tracks: "Love that speaks to me in my
mind." He turns and sees that the song is coming from his
Florentine friend Casella, a celebrated musician who is now
marching up the penitential slopes. Dante pauses, enraptured
by the melody and spellbound by the cadence.

A thunderous voice interrupts his reveries: "What is this,
laggard spirits? / What's this negligence, why this delay?" The
gatekeeper of Purgatory, old Cato, white-bearded dispenser of
justice from ancient Rome, has come to shatter Dante's trance
and remind him of the climb ahead.

One of Dante's greatest readers, T. S. Eliot, also captured
what it feels like when we encounter a work of art that we love.
In a poem indebted to Dante, "The Love Song of J. Alfred
Prufrock," Eliot writes:

We have lingered in the chambers of the sea
By sea-girls wreathed with seaweed red and brown
Till human voices wake us, and we drown.

In my grief I identified more closely with Dante than ever
before, especially his story of exile, the feeling of being a pilgrim
suddenly adrift in a dark wood. But *The Divine Comedy* was not
a self-help manual, a means to a practical set of ends that I was
able to negotiate based on Dante's advice. To say as much would
do violence to the kind of poem that Dante tried to write. In my
grief his words cast a spell, just as Dante himself was entranced

by Casella's song. Reading *The Divine Comedy*, we pause on the journey we're supposed to be taking. We linger by poetry's beautiful sea-girls wreathed in red and brown. The poem distracts us as much as it instructs us. But in that distraction—that pause on whatever purgatorial climb we may find ourselves—the closed fist of our heart begins to unclench.

Amor che ne la mente mi ragiona. Love that speaks to me in my mind. Casella's song captures what it's like to be grieving over someone you love. The conversation isn't between you and anyone else; it's between you and yourself, the circular talk of memories. Maybe Freud was right. To get your libido back, to affix it to a living body, you first have to stop treating shades as solid things.

A FEW DAYS BEFORE CHRISTMAS 2008 and just three months after our first date, Astrid and I met in the tennis club of her hometown, Edelweiss, a stucco-and-timber village out of the Grimm Brothers in the southwestern German region of Swabia. I had flown out to spend the holidays with her and her family while Isabel remained behind in Rhode Island with my mom and sisters. Our relationship had been heading toward this match ever since our meeting at Bar Boulud. That day in New York she had shown up for lunch with her daughter slung around her neck, all smiles and hello, before asking the fateful question that would ultimately undermine us: "Is Isabel with you?"

She had met Isabel on several different occasions, and expected her to come with me to Germany, as she had every right to. But Astrid didn't realize just how settled my situation in Westerly had become. After more than a year into our journey of child rearing, the routines and responsibilities had cemented, as my family and I formed the unlikeliest of teams: my mother, Yolanda, widowed at age sixty-four after fifty years of marriage; the eldest daughter, Margaret, who lived a thousand feet from my mom and visited her every day, and who had been a second mother to me growing up; the middle girls, Mary and Rose, the closest to me in temperament and taste, women who themselves would have been artists or writers or teachers had my father, a Calabrian taskmaster from the oldest of old schools, allowed them to have a proper education; and my youngest sister, Tina, whose two children had become Isabel's best friends and who lived across the street from my mom in a house built on one of the plots of land that my father had paid for with twenty-five years of backbreaking factory work. The eldest child, my brother Angelo, prematurely retired because of health problems, played the messenger Hermes to my mother's Hera, queen of the Calabrian gods, checking in each day to see if diapers were needed from CVS or coffee from Dunkin' Donuts. Just the sight of his white Mazda chariot was enough to cheer me up: his was the lone male presence in an otherwise *villaggio femminile*.

The world that I had pledged to abandon for good when I left home at age eighteen for college was now the very life in which I ensconced my infant daughter. My sisters were increasingly mystified by my incapacity to drop everything to look after my baby. They were discovering that their seemingly good-natured and easygoing younger brother was a Calabrian *testa dura*, "hard head," after all, and he had gotten it into his thick skull that he wanted his former life back, with new love and companionship. They had come to see me as incapable of submitting to the drudgery of child care.

And that is how I saw it and what I couldn't face: the drudgery. The grinding rhythms of focusing exclusively on a child. My child. *Our* child. That was supposed to be Katherine's job. I felt both ill equipped and unwilling. Stubborn, even. It was not supposed to be this way. Never once did I ask myself what would have been my part in caring for Isabel if Katherine were still alive. I couldn't get that far in my thinking. Instead, I would disappear for three days every week to return to Bard and my teaching, and when I was back in Rhode Island for long weekends with Isabel, I let my mother change her diapers, get up with her in the middle of the night, and wash the sweat and tears off her body. Whenever I traveled to visit a friend or give a talk, I did so without Isabel. My mother and sisters were nervous about her traveling with me, which only validated my nervousness at the prospect of bringing her along.

For the Luzzi women, child care was not a natural male habitat. They had no expectation that I would don a Baby-Björn and attune myself to the rhythms of an infant; they hoped only that when I watched Isabel I would keep her alive until they showed up. When I offered my own ideas on what seemed right in raising her—that she eat healthy food, be read to, go to kiddie music classes—they scoffed at my yuppie notions. My year of playing a weak male copilot to these female Calabrian captains destroyed what little will I had to parent on my own.

Then came the wonder of Astrid. A woman who had lost her love, who like me was given a gift to mitigate her mighty despair—a girl no less, Isabel's twin in the rarest parallel. There is no report card issued at the death of a beloved spouse, yet I sensed immediately that Astrid was holding up better than me. She and Anja were letting Isabel and me in, but only up to a point. Astrid knew that it was too soon for her, for both of us—she might as well have been channeling my grief counselor, Rosalind, on this point—to think about building something together. We were both in the basement of grief, and she was wise enough to enjoy the cool air.

That winter day in Edelweiss, Astrid wore white tennis shorts and red sneakers, and from the first thwack of the ball, I could tell that she played to win. We were up against her sister and brother-in-law from Hamburg, who had made the journey for some hyper-Germanic Christmas celebrations, complete with a church performance of Bach's *Christmas Oratorio* and a family reunion with *Kaffee und Kuchen*, the family apartment redolent of thickly buttered strudel and stollen. To me this made things official: Astrid and I were a doubles team, on our way to becoming a couple. It was hard to believe, just a year after Katherine's death and I was being given a second chance at love, so soon after the close of the first. Here was the proof: Astrid's banker brother-in-law, with perfect European form, snapped a serve into my deuce court, I floated back a slice to Astrid's sister, who cracked a forehand crosscourt to Astrid, who bent her knees for a forehand back to her brother-in-law, who wound up for a classic one-handed topspin backhand. We were all inhabiting the point, but I saw it much differently from the others. They saw a respectable recreational rally, but I watched the ball connect me to a new family as it traced the lines of a *vita nuova* in the air.

These were lines, in the magical thinking of my grief-clouded mind, that I imagined had been drawn long ago, in World War II and in a memory I clung to, if only to convince myself further that Astrid and I were destiny's children.

In 1946, in the fields of Bavaria not too far from Astrid's town, my father married a German woman who loved him more than he loved her. He did it to save his own skin. She was the niece of *il maresciallo*, the marshal, a municipal official who ran the farm where my father had been sentenced to enforced labor after his Italian army switched sides in 1943, abandoning Hitler's Nazi-led Axis. He would eventually leave his German wife when she was pregnant and escape back to his native Calabria, where within months he would meet my mother—a woman he truly did love.

The roles were now reversed. His son had fallen for a German woman who needed him less than he needed her. A woman who was looking for a human companion while he was looking for a human tourniquet.

Because of all the tennis I'd been playing, Astrid and I beat her sister and brother-in-law, but not without a fight. It was one of the few victories, and certainly the most memorable, of my time with Astrid.

If only things could have stopped there.

VIRGIL, DANTE'S GUIDE IN THE first two canticles of the afterlife, knew a thing or two about love affairs that stopped soon after starting. Dissatisfied with the *Aeneid*, the book that occupied the last ten years of his life, he left instructions in his will for it to be burned upon his death. Had his wish been granted, this act would have deprived posterity of what is arguably the single greatest poem ever written before Dante's *Divine Comedy*. Thankfully, there was a reader of Virgil who was above the law—because he *was* the law: the Emperor Augustus, who rescued the *Aeneid* from the flames and ordered its publication. This ruler of the not-so-free world had commissioned Virgil's epic poem on the mythic founding of Rome. He had heard Virgil recite portions of it, and he savored the references to him and his people as descendants from the gods. But he didn't understand that much of the *Aeneid* actually undermined the things he stood for as supreme ruler of Rome and its vast empire. For Virgil realized that the glory of Rome was reflected in a pool of blood. Francesca da Rimini was willing to die for love; Virgil's hero Aeneas was willing to let love die for politics.

After the Greeks burn Troy to the ground, Aeneas sets sail to look for a new home for his people. Eventually he makes landfall in the thriving North African city of Carthage, filled with workers buzzing like bees. That's the sound that Aeneas knows and loves best: the hum of duty. It arrests him—just as, early in *Purgatorio*, Dante had been halted in his tracks by the music of his old friend Casella. When he lost Troy, Aeneas also lost his wife, Creusa. She had been walking behind him, but when he turned and looked, she had disappeared. He hurled himself back into the burning city to find her, only to encounter her shade: go on, she tells him in effect, fulfill your destiny, found your city, marry your royal bride. Someone from your village. And stop treating shades as solid things. Aeneas escapes from Troy with his father, Anchises, on his shoulders, and his young son, among other survivors.

The African queen he meets in Carthage, Dido, is all too solid. She falls for the handsome, dutiful warrior at first sight—aided along by one of Cupid's arrows. She yearns to hear his story. "Sorrow, unspeakable sorrow, / my queen, you ask me to bring to life once more," strong, silent Aeneas tells her—a phrase that reminds us of Francesca's words to Dante in *Inferno*, when she tells him how bitter it is to look back on her past from her position of woe. Dante actually places Dido alongside Francesca in the Circle of the Lustful in hell. But he misunderstood Dido's true love, which was filled with compassion and free from the impulses that landed sinners in Inferno's fires. And Aeneas falls for Dido just as hard as she does for him. How could he not? She was beautiful, brilliant, and she listened to each of his words with yearning and compassion.

He spills his heart to his tender listener, feasts at her table, and enjoys an afternoon hunt with her. One afternoon, they descend alone together into a cave. By the end of the day they are man and wife.

The gods are now terrified, worried that Aeneas will tarry in the comforts of this African love nest and abandon his quest for Rome—in the land of the city's eternal enemy, no less. So they send down Mercury, who tries to talk some sense into the hero:

> . . . *You, so now you lay*
> *foundation stones for the soaring walls of Carthage!*
> *Building her gorgeous city, doting on your wife,*
> *Blind to your own realm, oblivious to your fate!*

Oblivious to your fate. Few are destined, like Aeneas, to found an empire. But there's another way to look at Mercury's words. He's saying, *mogli e buoi dei paesi tuoi.* Marry someone from your hometown. Just as his late wife Creusa suggested to him before disappearing into the flames of Troy. *If you stay in Carthage, Aeneas,* Mercury hints, *you'll be like Ulysses in Calypso's cave: a man far from his true home, his metaphysical village.*

Aeneas digests Mercury's words and prepares to leave in secret. But Dido catches him on the shore, accusing him of abandoning her like a thief in the night.

"*Italiam non sponte sequor,*" he responds. "I set sail for Italy—all against my will."

It's a lame excuse, but it's true. And yet Dido needs more from Aeneas, some rage, something to show that if he must go, it's with a broken heart. But it's too late. Aeneas has already lost everything—remember, he watched his city burn to the ground and lost his wife Creusa in the fire. As with Dante and Ulysses, his fate is eternal, internal exile. He holds his tongue. Dido storms off, telling Aeneas that she will curse him and his future race of Romans forever.

In her anguish, Dido instructs her sister Anna to build a fire in her courtyard so that she can burn all of Aeneas's things, including the bed they had slept on. As Aeneas's ship pulls out of the harbor, Dido hurls herself onto the fire, making a funeral pyre out of what was supposed to have been the cleansing flames, plunging Aeneas's sword into her womb.

I shall die unavenged, but die I will! . . .
And may that heartless [Aeneas], far at sea,
drink down deep the sight of our fires here
and bear with him this omen of our death!

These are Dido's last words.

"YOU HAVE ONE PROBLEM," ASTRID is saying to me in one of Edelweiss's medieval taverns after our tennis match. "A *big* one."

"Oh yeah, and what is that?"

"You know what it is."

I do know, but I can't admit it to myself because it's too shameful. Even when Astrid utters the word in her German accent, *Issa-bel*, hissing the *S* just as Ulysses had hissed his flaming words to Dante in hell, I fall into the usual defensive stance and channel kind and well-intentioned Rosalind.

I'm doing the best I can, I say. *It's not an easy situation, and I don't have all the answers. Isabel is getting a ton of love. I'm just trying to get back on my feet.*

Maybe it's because I'm in Germany and everyone else is speaking a different language, or maybe it's because I'm tipsy from the beer, but my words sound rehearsed and hollow.

Shortly after our time in Germany, Astrid and I met in San Francisco for the Modern Language Association's annual convention. For the first and last time, it was just the two of us, as Anja was with Astrid's mother in Germany and Isabel was as usual with my family in Rhode Island. We ate rabbit at Chez Panisse in Berkeley. We drove across the Golden Gate Bridge. She met my West Coast friends. We made love in the afternoon in the conference's corporate hotel, the curtains drawn and a DO NOT DISTURB sign affixed to the door amid the swirl of postcolonial panels and Victorianist cash bars. Each morning I went down to pick up coffee and yogurt for our breakfast from the Hyatt Starbucks. I wore a baseball cap to cover my disheveled hair and a blazer to hide my crumpled T-shirt. As the elevator descended the concrete slabs, I daydreamed about the Christmas season in Germany, sure that Astrid and my mixed doubles victory in Edelweiss had been the start of something.

Then we took a car ride on New Year's Eve.

ON DECEMBER 31, 2008, ASTRID and I checked out of our convention hotel in San Francisco and headed to Sonoma to celebrate with friends of hers at a cabin in the mountains, a setting that could not have been more romantic. Along the way we passed through small rural towns selling organic baked goods and fair-trade coffee, and we stopped frequently to wrap ourselves around each other, bask in the sun, gossip about colleagues. By all appearances we were a couple. Everything fit, our height and hair, the careers and family values—to an outsider we might have looked as though we were on our honeymoon or anniversary. That car ride to Sonoma was as close as we ever came to being a couple—which only made its shocking counterpoint, the car ride from Sonoma, all the more befuddling.

After an awkward New Year's Eve—whenever we were around her friends, Astrid's misgivings about our relationship expressed themselves in an embarrassed lack of affection for me—we climbed back into our rental car, the love mobile that had transported us from San Francisco. But as the car made its way toward the airport everything changed. Astrid was about to move from New York to start a job as an adjunct professor in a Midwestern college. She had a week to pack up her apartment and arrange preschool and child care for her daughter in a completely new city for them both. She insisted on doing it without my help. The reality of what she was facing settled in. The holidays, first in Germany then in California, had been a lovely interlude for Astrid. But now she had work to do, a daughter to protect, a new life to build. She had seen that doubles rally in Edelweiss differently than I had. While Astrid had been happy to have me on the same side of the court, she would have been just as content to play singles. It was I who couldn't bear the thought of trading groundstrokes alone.

After dropping off our rental car, we ate burritos in silence in the San Francisco airport and prepared to board our separate planes: I to Providence en route to Westerly and my mother and sisters, my Little Calabria; she to La Guardia and the Brooklyn loft that she and Jorge had built together. To the place that she and Anja called home.

DIDO AND AENEAS WILL MEET again—after Dido's death.

After abandoning the Carthaginian queen, Aeneas visits the Underworld to receive the prophecy of his destiny from his late father, Anchises. Along the way he sees the ghost of Dido, "shadowy among the shadows"—ghostlike even among fellow shades. Finally, Aeneas gives her the one thing Dido had asked of him: an honest explanation.

"I swear by the stars," he says to her, "I left your shores, my [queen], against my will. Yes, / the will of the gods . . . drives me through the shadows now."

In hell, it's always someone else's fault—the gods for Aeneas, love for Francesca, fate for Ulysses. After Aeneas speaks, Dido turns away with her eyes fixed on the ground. Without so much as a word to the man she died for, she flees to her late husband,

Sychaeus, the man whom she had loved before Aeneas. He absorbs her suffering, "meets her love with love."

Meets her love with love. The one thing that Aeneas could not provide because he didn't understand that to love someone truly—not just attach your libido to her, as Freud would say— you have to be willing to give things up, even your duty to the gods.

By the end of the *Aeneid*, Aeneas finally gets what he wants: he marries a royal lady, someone from his metaphysical village, the blandly beautiful Lavinia, and founds an imperial city by vanquishing the native tribes in what would become Rome. But in the book's final scene—in an ending that must have made Dante jealous—we see duty's terrible effect on Aeneas. Just before dispatching his mortal enemy Turnus, Aeneas loses his mind over the sight of his friend Pallas's armor on Turnus's shoulders, which Turnus had taken as a spoil of war after killing Pallas:

> *. . . flaring up in fury,*
> *terrible in his rage, [Aeneas] cries: "Decked in the spoils*
> *you stripped from one I loved—escape my clutches? Never—*
> *Pallas strikes this blow, Pallas sacrifices you now,*
> *makes you pay the price with your own guilty blood!"*

You see, it's not me, who's doing this, he's saying, *it's . . . Pallas. As pleased another,* to use the words of Dante's Ulysses. Aeneas can accept responsibility neither for abandoning Dido nor slaying Turnus. This is why Dante placed Francesca in hell, and why Dido refused to even speak to Aeneas: because the damned always refuse to accept responsibility for their actions and embrace that greatest gift of all, free will.

It's very easy, in the midst of your grief and mourning, to think that you've lost your free will. After all, you're a victim of fate—just like Ulysses, who watches helplessly as a violent storm drowns him and his crew. But part of the process of getting back on your feet again is to realize that there are in fact parts of your life that you must reclaim. I understood this right away when it came to my career, as I clung to my work after the rest of my life had been shattered. For Dante, free will was an especially valuable quality because his world was one where God saw and knew all—and yet, Dante also believed, within this divine structure the individual still had the freedom to create his own life's path. The dialogue between this individual freedom and a well-ordered Christian universe made free will into the ultimate gift—and burden—for humankind. For me, free will would entail embracing the new roles that death had foisted upon me—single parent, widower—with the same energy and creativeness with which I was pursuing my career. But those two roles were much more daunting, even frightening, than the familiar realms of teaching and scholarship, and so I held on to what I knew, with the ferocity of Francesca embracing Paolo's weightless body, rather than venturing out from the comfort of things I could control.

Dante needs to understand free will before he can leave Purgatory—and his guide Virgil knows it. In a stunning garden atop Mount Purgatory, and after sixty-one cantos together, Dante and Virgil stood at the entrance to the Garden of Eden, the last stop before heaven. Theirs has been the strangest of literary friendships, an intimate bond shared between a medieval Christian and ancient pagan separated by a millennium. Mesmerized by Beatrice's approaching chariot, Dante barely heard his beloved guide speak:

> . . . *The temporal and eternal fire*
> *you have seen, my son, and now come to a place*
> *that is beyond my vision.*

Then Virgil speaks for the final time in the poem, bestowing upon Dante the one thing he could never gain for himself:

Your will is free, upright, and whole, Virgil tells Dante. *I crown you and miter you the ruler of yourself.*

Free will: the one thing you need before you can love again. Virgil has given Dante, in his own words, *"lo maggior don,"* the greatest gift.

FOR A FEW MONTHS I pretended that things between Astrid and me hadn't ended with the car ride from Sonoma and the burritos at San Francisco International Airport. I went to see her at her new job in the Midwest; she continued to hold me tight at night as my chest throbbed into hers; I kept on telling her I was in over my head. But I could feel her slipping away, already committed to a life that did not include me.

We tried to make plans but always ended up fighting—putting ourselves, as Astrid would say, in a "predicument," her slight mispronunciation lending the word an awful Teutonic authority.

"We can have the dream," she said to me, "my Brooklyn apartment as a base while we pursue our careers elsewhere. We'll see each other as often as possible. I know we can make this work."

But I knew that this meant life on her terms, in the loft that she had shared in Cobble Hill with Jorge, a brilliant designer who had transformed their small one-bedroom into something suitable for a magazine spread. This was her American Dream, the urban living that had drawn her away from her cozy German village. I argued that we should live closer to Bard and the Hudson Valley: I was tenured, I would try to negotiate a position for her. We could renovate a farmhouse, I coaxed her, we would have all the organic food you could shake a farm stand at—open fields for our girls to run around in, small-batch syrup and honey to thrill the gods. I wanted her on my terms, just as she wanted me on hers. We could not work toward any middle ground because there was none between us. In the end, what we shared was a story—one powerful and moving enough to hold us together for many months, but ultimately helpless against the heavy lifting of day-to-day life. We had PhDs, but we did not like the same kinds of books; we had infant daughters, but we wanted to raise them differently; we had lost our spouses, but we stood worlds apart on what that absence meant to us. I was anxious to reclaim the half of my life that death had taken. Astrid was complete with herself and her child.

A few months after our mixed doubles and burritos, I showed up in New York City to spend the week with Astrid during our spring break. When I walked in the apartment, she wasn't smiling. She met me in the doorway, blocking my entrance, with the same question she had posed in Bar Boulud six months earlier: "Where's Isabel?" Instead of answering her question, I threw up my usual verbal Maginot Line.

"Isabel's fine—she's home with my family, where she belongs."

"No, Isabel belongs *here*—with you, with us. You can't see that."

"I can't see it because you won't let me see anything that you don't want me to. You want us here on *your* terms, not ours."

And so on. We spent the next forty-eight hours arguing about my inability to cut the cord with my family and raise Isabel on my own, her refusal to let me and Isabel inside her and Anja's life, and my inability to understand why she needed to have something for herself outside of "us" (which was another way of saying: my inability to understand why she couldn't be more like Katherine). Anja cried nonstop the entire visit, as if the acid chemistry between Astrid and me were making her ill. Two days into what was supposed to have been our week together, I boarded a train at Penn Station to head back to Westerly and Isabel. Exhaustion had pushed us into mutual surrender: we agreed that things between us were finally and irrevocably over. As the train eased out of New York and along the familiar Connecticut coastline—the industrial sorrow of Bridgeport, the rusted bridges of New London, the gorgeous inlets of Mystic—I felt deeply alone. But I was too tired to be sad, and when the train pulled into Rhode Island, my heart throbbed with joy at the thought of being reunited with Isabel. Astrid had been right: I *did* have one big problem, and it wasn't my love life. I hadn't yet found the key to the biggest challenge that grief had given me, the biggest challenge of my life: how to rebuild my world around Isabel without the help of my family. I didn't have the answer to this question on that warm and cloudless March day, but at least I was no longer kidding myself that the magic German woman, the one I had fantasized about for months before meeting up and falling in love with her—could wave her wand at my broken life and snap it back into form, as elegantly as her brother-in-law had cracked his exquisite one-handed backhands. I was alone now, to be sure. But at least I was no longer under the spell of magical thinking.

When I stepped off the train in Westerly, for the first time since Katherine's death, the air no longer felt electric.

CHAPTER 5

The Gears of Justice

I s this the address of Joseph Luzzi?"

I had heard this official, blandly menacing tone before—when the security guard had come to find me on the third floor of Bard's Olin Hall a year earlier, on November 29, 2007, the morning of Katherine's accident. The guard had only asked me my name, but it was enough to send me running down the stairs and into another life. On this night, however, there was nowhere to run. I was spending a rare weekend in Tivoli with Isabel: my sisters Mary and Rose had brought her over from Rhode Island, and I had just put her to sleep in the room that was to have been her nursery. The man at the door was carrying papers. He told me in well-rehearsed words that I was "being served," the passive voice absolving him from any responsibility. Katherine's estate was being sued, and I, as its executor, was named on the suit. With my life still in pieces, I was now being plunged into the maddening depths of a lawsuit—instigated, no less, by the driver of the car who killed my wife, Eddie Knight, who was seeking compensation for injuries sustained in the accident. If there was any single event in the aftermath of Katherine's death that almost broke me, it was this. I heard that voice saying *hang on*, but it was getting more and more faint, as I signed the line acknowledging that I was in fact Joseph Luzzi.

LA BOCCA SOLLEVÒ DAL FIERO pasto.

"He lifted up his mouth from the savage meal"—when my uncle Giorgio recited these words thirty years ago, it marked the start of my lifelong journey with Dante Alighieri, Italy's greatest writer. On the long train ride back to Florence from Calabria, I silently repeated Giorgio's words as I imagined the Pisan Count Ugolino gnawing on the skull of his enemy, Archbishop Ruggieri, in the Circle of Treachery, the ninth and lowest ring of hell. In March 1289, and on Ruggieri's orders, Ugolino and his family were thrown into Pisa's notorious Hunger Tower. A few days later, at the hour their food was usually brought to them, Ugolino and his children heard a resounding thud: the pounding of nails to seal the entry to the tower. No more food or water. The children could take it no longer: "Father, it would pain us much less," they begged, "if you would eat from us: you clothed us / in this miserable flesh, now strip it off." Within six days, all four of his children starved to death. Blind with grief and hunger, Ugolino stumbled and groped over their corpses, calling for them—but they were already dead. By the seventh day he too was broken:

Poscia, più che 'l dolor, potè 'l digiuno.

Then hunger had more power than grief.

We may never know for sure whether or not Ugolino ate his children—Dante's line about "hunger having more power than grief" is difficult to pin down to a specific meaning. And Ugolino is technically in hell for treason, not cannibalism. But I believe that he did eat them. Dante's poetry, with its cannibalistic images, suggests as much, as does his system of justice: engaged in cannibalism for eternity, Ugolino must have committed a related crime during his lifetime. Exiled in his prime because of a deal hatched between his political rivals and Pope Boniface VIII, Dante understood that perfect, divine law could exist only in the pages of his *Divine Comedy*. This distance between human law and absolute justice is the main theme of his *Inferno*.

Ugolino's dark words reveal the principle of justice in Dante's hell: the sin becomes the punishment. When Dante meets Bertran de Born, an agitator who divided the king from his subjects, he carries his own severed head in his arms and announces, *"Così s'osserva in me lo contrapasso"*—"So you see in me the counter-passion." By counter-passion, Dante meant that the same force that created the sin comes back to act as its punishment. In God's world, justice is absolute and mathematically precise.

I had made it out of hell and into purgatory, and—with that stroke of the pen acknowledging that I was indeed Joseph Luzzi—I was about to experience my own version of the eternal struggle between human law and true justice.

"THE GEARS OF JUSTICE GRIND very slowly."

My attorney, Aaron Arweld, said these words to me in a café near the Dutchess County Courthouse in Poughkeepsie, just a few miles from where Katherine died and Isabel was born. It was now November 2010, two years after I had been named in a suit against Katherine, and three years after her accident. I had waited until the final moment—literally the last days legally possible—to file a suit of my own against the driver who had struck her. My family had been urging me for years to do it.

Isabel has lost everything, they would say, *she deserves something in return. Money won't bring Katherine back, but . . .*

Yet I was paralyzed. I couldn't bring myself to do battle with the anonymous man who had been driving the fatal van. I owed it to Isabel to get as much as I could on her behalf. Nobody would deny that what had happened to Isabel and me was a tragedy. But then practical needs steered the actions of everyone connected to the accident: the driver seeking compensation; the insurance companies, which did not want to loosen their purse strings; the lawyers, who either wanted to win money or keep it from being won; and my family, who wanted Isabel to secure her future, at least financially. Everybody was playing his or her role except me. After three years of hemming and hawing, I finally surrendered to what I imagined to be the logic of responsible parenting and filed suit. As I signed the papers in Arweld's midtown Manhattan office, I felt like vomiting.

Arweld was a compact, likeable man whose wife had taught history at a college near Bard, so he understood my academic world. We were immediately simpatico, and he put me to work. My tasks included sending him pictures of the crash site, speaking with his assistant about the case, and filling out the endless forms that go into a lawsuit. I soon discovered the painful and painstaking slowness of litigation. Despite my initial frustration with how long the gears of justice took to grind, I eventually came to admire the suit's sluggish logic and glacial pace, which eroded the possibility of unchecked emotional reactions.

"You just never know what will happen," Arweld repeated his pet phrase to me as he picked at his Danish.

Decades of witnessing unexpected verdicts by juries and unanticipated decisions by judges had made him more philosophical about human nature than anyone I had ever met on a college humanities faculty. He had seen it all—until now: a woman struck by a vehicle and who then delivered a child before succumbing. We were on legally uncharted ground. The only thing we could be sure of was that the insurance companies would not want to pay out, and the defending attorneys would do everything to keep them from paying.

So I sat and filled out forms.

DANTE TOO HAD DEALT WITH his share of legal documents. He signed the edict in 1300 banishing Guido Cavalcanti, choosing justice over friendship. He raged over Florence's decree in 1302 that he be burned alive if he returned to the city. And when he finally sat down in 1305 to write *The Divine Comedy*, the question of justice was his first concern—especially when he thought of Brunetto Latini.

Ser (or "Sir") Brunetto was a brilliant scholar born around 1220, a generation before Dante. When his Guelph party lost to the Ghibellines in the historic Battle of Montaperti in 1260, Brunetto decided to stay in France, where he had been on a diplomatic mission. While there he wrote an encyclopedic poem, *The Treasure*, which taught the foundations of rhetoric and humanistic learning. He was among the first intellectuals in the Middle Ages to urge a return to Greco-Roman culture, that same pagan worldview, embodied by Dante's guide Virgil, that would pave the way for the European Renaissance. It's unclear whether Dante actually knew Brunetto or just his writings; either way, Brunetto's words taught Dante how, as he writes in *Inferno*, "*l'uom s'etterna*"—"man makes himself eternal."

Brunetto's presumed homosexuality landed him in Dante's Circle of the Sodomites. There's actually no record of his orientation or whether he engaged in sexual activity that Dante's Catholic Church would have condemned, and scholars continue to argue today about what specific transgression Dante was thinking of when he decided to place Brunetto in Inferno's burning sands. Whatever the reason, it's not Brunetto's alleged sin that troubles Dante when they meet in hell: it's how Brunetto believes that outside forces, even chance, landed him in hell, and that he himself is blameless.

Spying Brunetto in the burning sands of hell, Dante tenderly asks, "Are *you* here, Sir Brunetto?" to which his teacher replies: "O my son . . . / . . . what fortune or destiny / brings you down here before your final day, / and who is this that shows you the way?" Dante is quick to answer: "Up there, in the happy life / . . . I lost my way in a valley, / before my time was up."

In the middle of our life's journey, Dante is basically saying, *I found myself in a dark wood.* Moving words, especially from a former student—but Brunetto is not listening. Soon after meeting Dante, he lapses into a rage, fulminating against the Florentines—"*quello ingrato popolo maligno,*" "that ungrateful and malignant people"—and warning Dante that he too will suffer the fallout from Florence's poisonous politics. The people in hell love the sound of their own voices, and Brunetto is no different. Instead of commiseration, or a kind word of advice, the charred Brunetto continues to pontificate: "If you follow your star," he famously tells Dante, "you cannot fail to reach a glorious port."

Fate, stars, destiny. Brunetto evokes the laws of chance that

Dante is learning to overcome with his free will. What's more, Dante is trying to empty himself of the hatred that made his first years of exile the lowest point in his life. The sight of his former teacher cursing the Florentines moves Dante to pity. We wonder if he will faint again, just as he did with Paolo and Francesca. But he is farther along in his journey, and gives one of his first mature speeches in the poem. "If my prayer were answered," Dante says to Brunetto, "you would not yet / be banished from humanity." Dante is done with worrying about the whims of fortune—he wants to move beyond human law and reach a higher understanding of good and evil. His words suggest that he will always love Brunetto. But it's time to say good-bye to him.

"Let my book *The Treasure*, in which I still live on, / be dear to you—I ask for nothing more," Brunetto says to him as they part. We've all heard these words before: *It's so wonderful to hear your news, but let me tell you about* me. . . . Like so many sinners in hell, Brunetto is proud of his own words, incapable of listening to others.

Then [Brunetto] turned back, and he seemed like one
of those who race for the green cloth
in the fields of Verona—and he looked more like
the one who wins than the one who loses.

Each year in Dante's lifetime a race was held outside Verona. All the participants were naked, and the winner received a green cloth, the loser a crowing cock. Is Brunetto the winner or loser? It's impossible to say.

By the time of the lawsuit, I understood that I was a victim and that I had done nothing wrong to merit the terrible reality of Katherine's death. But I was still paralyzed by my sense of having failed Isabel and not risen to the occasion of being her sole care provider. And in failing Isabel I felt that I was failing Katherine, not living up to the responsibility of the gift she had left me with. I was doing battle with my mighty opponent, grief, and, like Brunetto, it was impossible to tell whether I was moving forward or running naked in the wrong direction.

IN 2011, DEEP INTO THE quagmire of my lawsuit, Arweld sent me a form from a company called InterAnalytics. The document sought to establish the monetary value of Katherine's life and our relationship, which Arweld would then use in the lawsuit. The blasé, almost bored tone of the document and its puritanical sense of propriety floored me. It asked me to list things that Katherine and I had done together—the hobbies and interests we shared, a typical day together—as if I were filing a tax return or making a grocery list. My heart raced as I plugged in the data: coffee and breakfast in the morning before going our separate ways for work or school; meeting in the evening to cook dinner together and then take a walk or watch a movie. I felt as though someone was asking me to describe my beloved wife on a purely quantitative, statistical basis devoid of spirit—which in turn made Katherine's death feel more factual and heavy, a lifeless reality bereft of all hope. Mimicking the noxious precision of the document, I added that "weekend activities included taking long walks, shopping, visiting neighboring towns, going to the movies, and attending an arts-related event." But when I signed off in muted anger, I tried to humanize the document's dead letters: "As the above shows, my beloved late wife was my constant companion—and the best friend with whom I shared my most meaningful time."

Nowhere did it ask me how much I loved her or what her loss had meant, or even more telling matters like how often we argued or had sex. But then again, how could you quantify love? Even if you knew how often someone *made* love. Perhaps the questionnaire was wise to stick to appearances.

Meanwhile, my disgust over suing for money related to Katherine's death began to melt away, just as it had over my failing to protect her from death. Her loss grew heavier with each day, making it increasingly difficult to wallow in distracting what-ifs. Those hypotheticals were getting lost in my new frustrating reality: my emotional struggle to understand how to be a father to Isabel, my family's frustration with my absence in Isabel's life. All of which was made more challenging by a murderous weekly commute from Rhode Island to New York, and the lack of any friends in Westerly. The "facts"—to adopt the InterAnalytics lingo—were undeniable: I had truly suffered, was still suffering; Isabel had lost her mother; and we would live with this forever.

Since civil litigation was based on monetary compensation for damages incurred, then so be it, I thought: let's fight for what's rightfully ours.

The rational challenges posed by the lawsuit were helping me deal with Katherine's loss in other ways: my slow and reluctant acceptance of myself as victim was enabling me to plow ahead with the legal proceedings, while also treating myself with more kindness and understanding over the challenges of life as a widower and single parent. There's a legal phrase I learned, *res ipsa loquitur*, "the thing itself speaks," or, in effect, the facts speak for themselves—and the facts of Katherine's sudden death screamed that I would do well to heed Rosalind's words, to be patient about getting my life back together.

But, in legal terms, there was one problem—one *big* problem, as Astrid might say. The police report about the accident stated in no uncertain terms that Katherine should have waited for more of a break in the traffic before exiting the gas station. She had made a split-second judgment to try and merge with the traffic flow, and in the opinion of this report she had been mistaken. Arweld was undeterred.

"If it was only a question of police reports then we wouldn't need trials," he said time and again. "The report is just one opinion among many."

I agreed with him. In New York insurance law, legal blame for auto accidents is assigned on a percentage basis, with one hundred percent being total responsibility for the accident and zero percent no responsibility at all. I did not believe that my wife was one hundred percent responsible—that to me meant someone acting recklessly and without judgment, and that was not Katherine, a careful and defensive driver and an instinctively cautious and thoughtful person. Her decision had cost her life. But it did not in my opinion make her entirely at fault. There were too many other variables at play, and in my view whatever percentage of the accident was not her fault entitled us to make a claim for damages.

It wasn't all papers and percentages. As the second year dragged into the third and all the preliminary documents had been filed, the more adversarial aspects of the suit began to heat up. Including one that, for four years, I had been dreading.

"DO YOU WANT ME IN the room?" I asked.

"It's your decision," Arweld answered. "Completely up to you."

It was spring of 2012, and we were having lunch in a Greek diner in downtown Poughkeepsie close to the courthouse where we had filed suit two years earlier. That morning, I had given my deposition at the office of Knight's attorney. The deposition was as tedious and filled with legalese as the other documents I had been submitting. I kept waiting to hear those magic words that would end this slow-burning agony—"They want to settle"—but after my deposition I realized this was unlikely. The opposing side had the key to the kingdom: the official report from the New York State Police saying that Katherine should not have taken that turn. From his aggressive and pointed questioning, it was clear that the driver's attorney wasn't going to budge. At this stage in the case, Arweld and I were the plaintiffs and they the defendants; but it looked and sounded like *they* were on the attack and we under siege.

Mine wasn't the only deposition that morning. After I answered a slew of generic questions about Katherine's identity and our relationship, the big moment came: Knight's deposition. For years I had feared seeing him. He had become the bogeyman who set my grief and this legal wrecking ball in motion. He was my living link to the tragedy: if there was a single agent in my wife's disappearance from planet earth, he was it.

Knight had arrived for the deposition at the same time I did. I had pictured him in countless ways and, remarkably enough, he looked just as anticipated. He was a large, nervous man with a lumbering gait and tired eyes. The puffy face and wrecked body of someone who had been through the wringer. I avoided making eye contact as we consulted with our attorneys. My deposition was in the morning, his to follow in the afternoon.

As Arweld and I picked over our falafel at lunch before Knight's deposition, we discussed the pros and cons of my being in the room while he was deposed. On the one hand, Arweld reasoned, my being present might make Knight feel edgy and anxious and thus unable to deliver a clear statement, which would be bad for us. On the other hand, Knight's seeing me might make the reality of my wife's death—and his role in it—all the more palpable and work to our benefit.

"Either way," Arweld said, "it's your call."

As Virgil had said to Dante: now is the time to exercise your free will.

But I wanted an order from him, some clear-cut directive. Arweld was a decent and fair-minded man who would never insist one way or the other on what he knew was a judgment call—a situation in which my emotions were sure to be raw. The meal was ending, and we were sipping our coffees, about to return for Knight's deposition. Suddenly, Arweld perked up.

"Don't come in for Knight's deposition," he announced.

"Why not?" I asked.

He paused for a moment before answering.

"I don't want you having nightmares."

So much for my free will.

WHY DO YOU BREAK ME? Why do you rip me? Have you no sense of pity?

These sounds came from the inside of a tree whose branch Dante had snapped, releasing a splinter of bloody words. He was standing in the seventh circle of hell in the Wood of the Suicides, those who do violence to themselves. Soon he would watch his beloved Brunetto, emeritus professor of hell, speak from the heights in honeyed words. Now he was face to trunk with Pier delle Vigne—in a way, face to face with himself. Pier, like Dante, was a poet and politician, a self-made man. Born a century before Dante, he rose to prominence in the royal court of the Holy Roman Emperor Frederick II, the renowned ruler who earned the nickname *Stupor Mundi*, "the wonder of the world." Pier became the king's right-hand man:

> *I am the one who held both keys*
> *to Frederick's heart, and who turned them,*
> *locking and unlocking, so softly,*
> *that almost none could know his secrets.*

Pier tells Dante that his downfall was brought about by the plotting of jealous courtiers who falsely accused him of trying to poison Frederick, leading to his grisly end: Pier died in prison by dashing his brains against his stone cell. Dante listens to Pier's bitter words but cannot reply because of the pity that fills his heart. It was rumored that in the first years of Dante's exile from Florence, he was so poisoned by the desire for revenge that it almost led him to suicide. He nearly ended up in the same wood as Pier.

Dante pities Pier, but he doesn't absolve him. You can't absolve someone who does not accept responsibility for his actions. Again, in hell it's always somebody else's fault: Francesca blames her demise on love, Brunetto on Florence, Pier on his jealous rivals. In all of these cases, self-pity becomes the ultimate roadblock to self-understanding.

Two years into a lawsuit that consumed me with both self-pity and hatred for the man I blamed for Katherine's death, I felt the sting of Pier's lesson. Pier does not realize it, but the last thing he needs is for Dante to feel as sorry for him as he feels for himself.

In the long season after Katherine's death, self-pity became my constant companion. People would ask me how I was doing, and I would put on a brave face and say, "Fine, considering the circumstances," which were the right words with the wrong inflection. For I would pause between *fine* and *considering*, just enough to alert the careful listener that, actually, things couldn't be worse. One night, a colleague and his wife invited me to dinner at the Madalin Hotel near my apartment—the same place where I had savored duck and Sancerre with Astrid's friends just weeks after Katherine died.

"It's been amazing to see how open you've been about your feelings during all this," my friend said.

In his and his wife's eyes, I was definitely more the winner than the loser in my race with grief, and I wanted desperately to be seen as the one who would take suffering's green cloth in victory.

Something about the loss of my wife had seemed public from the start, in part because of the extraordinary circumstances surrounding it, and partly because of the tight-knit world it had occurred in. A friend of mine who called the Bard switchboard the day of Katherine's accident was shocked to get an update on the tragedy from the operator, as if the entire community were sharing in its effects. From the beginning, I felt the need to share my grief, hoping for comfort in the compassion of others. When Pier reaches out to Dante with his story—just as I offered mine to friends over glasses of wine and delicious entrées—he was hoping for Dante's pity to absorb his sorrow. But there are things that cannot be shared, and grief is one thing that you must endure ultimately alone, whether you're in the Wood of the Suicides or in a fancy country restaurant.

AARON ARWELD HAD BEEN DISSATISFIED with Knight's responses at the initial deposition, claiming that he was evasive, coached by his attorney, and unwilling to answer the questions. Our motion for a second deposition was accepted. This time Arweld gave me the order I'd been dreading:

"You need to be there. Knight needs to see your face."

I was ashamed to tell anybody this, but I was afraid. Facing Knight would mean facing the man who *killed my wife*, the large, fidgety man with the bloodshot eyes who was my sworn enemy. The man who had sued my late wife's estate—a grand word for someone with few earthly assets—less than a year after her death. In the intensity of my grief, I didn't ask myself what he himself had gone through because of the accident—what physical and emotional pain *he* had suffered, how it had affected his ability to work and carry on with what had been *his* former life, its effect on his sleep and his dreams. All I knew was that Knight's was the face that I attached to Katherine's death. Until the morning of his second deposition, I had never dared look him in the eye—including the morning of the first deposition, when I had avoided eye contact with him from the moment that he had lumbered into the office.

The forty-five-minute car ride from Tivoli to our new deposition was the longest of my life. Would Knight's face start to trouble my sleep, as Arweld had suggested it might? What would it be like to have an actual image now—a set of the jaw, a look in the eyes—to attach to the anonymous bogeyman that I'd been conjuring? I was about to confront the person who represented my sorrow as well as humanize the object of my anger.

For the poets of Dante's youth, love entered through the eyes, like mortal darts of light that sped right to the heart. I wondered if hatred also came in that way, as I pictured Knight's eyes emitting glaring shafts that would work their way inside me like invisible poison. As my car made its way past the green fields of Rhinebeck and the strip malls of Hyde Park, I felt as though I was finally going to confront the monster in the closet.

There was something even more disconcerting than Knight's face looming: a trial. Ours had all the markings of that tiny slice of civil suits that are not settled out of court. I agonized over the prospect of my wife's tragedy being hashed and rehashed in a Poughkeepsie courtroom, not far from where she died. Even if we ended up winning, that would not necessarily be the end, as the other side could appeal. The lawsuit felt endless—even as my grief was starting to fade into the long autumn of mourning.

All these thoughts swirling, I arrived in the courthouse and, for the first time ever, looked Knight in the eye.

DID DANTE CONSIDER TAKING HIS own life? The world will never know.

We do know that in those first years of exile he was so unhappy that he consorted with former enemies, people he called "mad and malignant" and would have otherwise disdained. We also know that he wandered from one Italian city to another looking for work as a diplomat or court intellectual: Forlì, 1302; Verona, 1303; Arezzo, Treviso, and Padua, 1305; Venice, Lucca, 1307–9. The map of Dante's wanderings is like a map of fragmented medieval Italy. He finally found a home in Verona at the court of Cangrande I della Scala, where he lived from 1312 to 1319 and wrote most of *The Divine Comedy*. His last city, Ravenna, also hosted him in relative peace from 1319 to his death in 1321, the year he wrote the last words of the *Comedy*. A distinguished Dante scholar once said that the poet had the good fortune of dying soon after completing his great poem—what could he have written after that?

Those are the dates, the facts and figures—the measurable things, just like the bloodless data I plugged into the InterAnalytics report asking about my life with Katherine. But what really went on inside Dante? For that, we have to look to his *sacro poema*. "He knew despair, and almost certainly contemplated suicide," writes the scholar Giuseppe Mazzotta. "But for all its harshness, exile turned out to be a blessing in disguise, no less than the central, decisive experience of his life." Once he had been exiled, Dante had to choose: remain stuck in self-pity, which would mean treating exile as a punishment, or work toward self-forgiveness, which would mean embracing exile as a liberation. Virgil had taught Dante that his greatest gift was free will; could he exercise it and transform the curse of exile into a blessing?

Outside Florence's historic center, on one of the city's tallest hills, stands the eleventh-century Basilica of San Miniato al Monte. I have trekked its stairs many times as it leads to a breathtaking view from atop the city at the Piazzale Michelangelo, with its massive reproduction of the *David* peering out over Florence's terracotta roofs. On a clear day you feel like you can reach out your hand and touch the tip of the Duomo, so close does the giant beehive of the cupola appear. I once heard a legend that, during those first years of his exile, Dante would supposedly walk to San Miniato and look upon his lost city. His home would seem close enough to touch, and for this reason all the more searing to miss.

Poring over the documents of my lawsuit, I would picture the poet on the hill of San Miniato looking out at Florence, his aquiline nose in profile, his face set in a lethally focused gaze. *It's all there*, I would think: *you can sense the salty taste of exile in that stare.* That feeling of living in places and with things that I never thought would be part of my world: the Rhode Island I thought I had left for good at eighteen, this lawsuit with its *whereas*es and *in accordance with*s. The accident had occurred in 2007, and here we were in 2012, five years later, with a constant and unresolved reminder of the dreadful day and its ongoing consequences. It was now all about money: who would pay, who would be paid, and how much the debits and credits would amount to. I kept telling myself that I was doing the right thing for Isabel, but part of me felt that no matter the amount of possible compensation, the mental and emotional strain was just not worth it. I felt confident enough that I would be able to work and save for my daughter and build a life for us even without this potential windfall, and I was desperate to be free from the legal albatross that reminded me of everything I had lost. Dante had supposedly looked out from San Miniato to Florence, back to the life he once had. The courtroom gave me a similar view, without the beauty of Florence's towers and domes to mitigate the nostalgia—as Francesca da Rimini would say—of looking back on happy times in ones of woe.

When we finally sat down for Knight's afternoon deposition, Arweld hammered away at him with a series of questions about his response to my wife's vehicle as she attempted to cross his lane and merge onto another road. The questions were repetitive, emphatic, and technical. Arweld was just doing his job, and doing it mighty well. But the drone of his words recalled all those legal documents I'd been filling out and their strangled locutions.

Knight's face wasn't so scary after all. It was, as I had gathered from my first glimpses, weary and agitated, but nothing that would cause nightmares. His eyes were blood-shot, but they were not threatening. The hardest thing about sitting through the deposition was not facing Knight; it was the tedium of the questions and answers, all those queries about turns taken, traffic lights perceived, brakes applied or neglected. After an hour as long and fragmented as my drive to Poughkeepsie with its nonstop red lights, the deposition ended.

Arweld was pleased.

"Having you here really made a difference," he told me afterward in the parking lot. "He saw you there, and it affected him."

I felt like I hadn't taken a full breath all day. Finally, on the ride home to Tivoli from Poughkeepsie I exhaled in relief. Knight's face was no longer that of a monster. His image now faded into something more benign. I still wanted to win the case: to clear up Katherine's name, to gain something for Isabel's future, to get closure on the whole legal episode. And I still believed that my wife was only partially responsible for the accident. But it struck me that this term described the case exactly: it was an accident.

We were in the delicate legal situation of needing to ascribe proportionate innocence or guilt in a situation where Katherine *and* Knight were victims. Knight had lived, my wife had not, but his life had clearly been forever altered by that random morning event, just as mine had. We were joined now in the aftermath of the tragedy. As I passed by the Franklin D. Roosevelt Presidential Library and made my way up Route 9, an unexpected feeling washed over me, one of empathy, even sympathy. Assigning blame was of no use to anyone—we all suffered and it mattered not the degree or percentage of either's culpability. I wanted to defeat him, but I no longer hated him. The last thing he would have expected or wanted that November morning in 2007 was to leave his house and hit and kill a young pregnant woman who died after giving birth. Yes, he had sued first, and that still angered me, but it did not cancel out his suffering.

SHORTLY AFTER KNIGHT'S SECOND DEPOSITION, our trial date was set for September 2012. Then, out of the blue, I received a phone call from Arweld. I thought it would be about some form I needed to fill out or some other technicality. But his voice was somber, and he had his colleague on the line for a conference call, the first time he had done this. He told me, with a mix of surprise and shock, that he had just received a notice from the judge assigned to our case. Based on the police report, she had accepted the defense's motion to dismiss our lawsuit against Knight. There would be no trial. The case was now closed.

The air left my lungs. I had been gearing up for the ugly attrition of the trial, which had become a black cloud hanging over every aspect of my slowly rebuilt life. And now suddenly it evaporated before my eyes.

In truth, the lawsuit's slow burn of anguish had ended weeks ago on the morning of Knight's second deposition when, driving home on Route 9G, I arrived at the exact spot where his van had struck and killed Katherine. Halted at the red light, the image of the black brake marks still seared in my memory, I was flooded with not only my and Katherine's suffering, but with Knight's own pain.

And, for the first time, utterly and unconditionally, I forgave him.

CHAPTER 6

Rough Draft

—————————————— ❧ ——————————————

Maybe I'll go to law school."

It was just hours after Katherine's death on November 29, 2007, and I was standing in Poughkeepsie's Vassar Brothers Hospital as I said these words to my sister Mary, both of us watching Isabel sleep amid the incubators of the neonatal unit. Mary's eyes widened in disbelief. *How,* her look of incredulity said, *can you be thinking of your career at a time like this?* But the thought didn't come from nowhere. For months before the accident, I had been waking up at five a.m. while Katherine slept to surf the web about part-time law programs. I loved my job as a professor of Italian—yet I felt that I should do more than spend my days teaching undergraduates how to order gelato in Rome or identify the mythological allusions in Petrarch. Perhaps it was hubris, even ungratefulness—after all, I was one of the lucky few, a tenured humanities professor in a science-obsessed world of underpaid adjuncts. I made a good living teaching and writing about Dante, and I cherished the classes I offered at Bard. Yet I sensed that my life would be incomplete if I remained in the ivory tower, no matter how sumptuous its Italianate stone.

I thought of my father who had left his family, friends, and beloved landscape in Calabria to immigrate to the United States, where he would work sixteen-hour days and die in exile. Was it all so I could have summers off and publish learned articles that used words like *diegetic* and *chiasmus*? A voice inside kept telling me, *live a life of meaning*. The day Katherine died, even in my shock, this was one of my first thoughts. Part of my impulse was to seek some sense of control in all of the chaos, and going to law school was something I could handle and direct, as opposed to the wild uncharted terrain of being a single father and widower. I spat out "law school" to my sister because this had always been my code for doing something in the more profitable "real world" outside of academe. But I knew the pipe dream of a law degree was just an illusory placeholder while I worked out my next career move. Katherine's death had occasioned ambition's perfect storm: I had always been a relentless and restless striver. Now, with Katherine gone, these old impulses were a way to numb and distract me from the day-to-day horrors of grief.

The dream of law school or something else like it was also part of another element of grief's magical thinking: the desire for a completely new start and new life after death, one completely different from the one I had known till then. The wrecking ball of death shatters your life down to its foundations, making it tempting to leave your ruined house altogether and build a new one elsewhere. In the fight-or-flight scenario that follows the sudden loss of your beloved, the appeal of another world far from the one you've just lost can seem infinitely more enticing than standing your ground and painstakingly trying to salvage the wreckage.

A month later, while driving to a family event on Christmas Day with my brother-in-law, I mentioned to him that I was considering a career in academic administration. But talk of becoming a dean, like that of becoming a lawyer, was just another way of expressing my doubt that teaching Italian language and literature was enough. As with law, I had no real intention of trading in the freedom and flexibility of my professor's job for the round-the-clock demands of the dean's office, even with its bump in salary. But there was that mantra—born out of self-doubt, perhaps, but made more salient after Katherine's death: *live a life of meaning.*

It was an impossibly generic, even clichéd exhortation. But I felt its empty phrasing trying to communicate to me in code, urging me to find the courage to live in a way that would do justice to Katherine's life and the love I felt for her. And the faith she had in me to live well and to the fullest.

After Beatrice's death, Dante stopped being the person he'd been—and it appalled those close to him, especially Guido, who wrote to Dante:

Each day I come to you endlessly,
Finding you with such low thoughts:
How I suffer at the loss of your gentle mind
And your abundant virtues.

Your grief over Beatrice, Guido tells Dante, is unhealthy— worse, it's vulgar. *Volgare.* For Guido, poetry was not meant to represent the normal run of life; it was supposed to be every- thing that our everyday life was not: lofty and ineffable. In writ- ing so movingly about Beatrice's death in the *Vita Nuova,* Dante used poetry to reflect on an all-too-common experience. He was filling the exquisite eliteness of Guido's poetry with press- ing human needs. That was Dante's gift—to merge the beauty of poetry with the visceral experiences of life, love, and death.

Dante was trying to live a life of meaning, and like any change on that order, it was going to shake up his world—even more than he'd anticipated.

WHEN I GRADUATED COLLEGE IN 1989 and moved to Paris, I survived by taking on a variety of odd jobs, from babysitter to bartender. I lived in a tiny *chambre de bonne,* a former maid's room, in an august building out of a Zola novel, and I rented the use of a shower from the Filipino maid who worked for my rich American landlords and lived down the hall from me. Mirra had left her husband and children back home in the Philippines while she worked in France and periodically sent them money. Her Filipino community of drivers, maids, and custodians took me in, inviting me to raucous Sunday parties in the servants' quarters of the city's most distinguished buildings, where they filled the musty eaves and cantilevered rooftops with gusts of cooking grease and waves of pounding dance music. There were even more cozy outings: one night, Mirra invited me and her friend Mohammed, an Algerian owner of a driving school, for dinner, and we ate fried chicken and Jell-O in the same room where I showered. That evening was the most comfortable I'd ever felt in the rarefied air of Paris's posh 7th arrondissement—a fitting place for Guido's elegant poetry if ever there was one.

My family was perplexed by my choice to move alone to Paris. While I told myself, and them, that I had gone there to learn French, the real story was that I moved to Paris to write. It was the ultimate cliché of literary exile: I would live in the city of light, as did Hemingway, Fitzgerald, Gertrude Stein, and Ezra Pound, and there I would write my first novel.

After a year in Paris, I had a draft of a novel, "The Joys and Sorrows of Tristan and Iseult," an adaptation of the medieval legend of the star-crossed lovers. I opted for the French spelling *Iseult* in deference to my adopted home and set the story in modern Paris. My Tristan was a pale and poetic young Frenchman, and Iseult a Parisian of southern Italian descent—a Ca- labrian family like my own. Tristan was the artsy blond kid I had always dreamed of being, and Iseult an idealized southern Italian version of myself. She too grew up in a northern land far from her parents' homeland, and like me, she was a survivor: Tristan dies tragically and unexpectedly toward the end of my novel, and Iseult finds the strength to endure. She would have had no problem begging for sausage and apples in Dresden.

When my French work permit expired, I traded in my roman- tic maid's room in Paris for a squalid bedsit in London. I spent my evenings there editing "Tristan and Iseult" after working during the daytime, first for a faith healer—Madame Antonia, who said she'd have both my legs broken if she found out I was throwing away her flyers instead of distributing them—then finally for a Labour Party fund raiser in a proper office job. By then, the romance of life abroad and its literary bohemia had faded. It's not easy being poor in London—unlike Paris, where all you need is a good loaf of bread, a bottle of Bordeaux, and the white light gleaming off the limestone buildings along the Seine. Gritty, industrial, and expensive, London was no place for dreams. The lack of sun was turning my skin gray, while the beer and cheap supermarket food, a mirthless rotation of ched- dar cheese and taramasalata, was making my waistline swell. By the time I finished editing my book I realized that I had not written a good novel or even a passable first one. And I was sick and tired of the endless delays on the London Underground's Northern Line and the Londoners' polite way of making me feel invisible. After two years abroad, I moved back to the U.S. and filed away my book—along with my dreams of becoming a novelist—in a desk drawer.

I spent several years in New York and kept on writing, publishing some short stories in my twenties, but in magazines too small even to merit the tag "little" (one actually misspelled my name as *Joesph*). By age thirty, I sealed shut my hopes of being a fiction writer in the same desk drawer that housed my novel. By then, I was in graduate school, having decided it would be wiser to write about books rather than make them up myself. I immersed myself in studying the authors I had always admired, especially those in the mighty Italian tradition that was part of my family's history—and especially the author I had leaned against all those years ago at the Basilica of Santa Croce in Florence. Meanwhile, I kept "Tristan and Iseult" under lock and key, erased the short stories from my CV, and added lines to a growing scholarly bibliography.

This is where Katherine found me in 2003.

IF YOU BELIEVE IN THE interchangeability of lovers, common sense would suggest that you should be able to fall in love again soon after you've lost your beloved—just as Guido moved from one dazzling lady to another. Guido was interested in how a lover made him feel, not the lover herself.

But if you believe in one deep, true love, common sense would also suggest that it would be difficult if not impossible to find another love of comparable intensity once your beloved is gone. Following this logic, we would guess that it would be hard for Dante to fall in love again after the death of Beatrice, an irreplaceable lady whom he mourned to the extreme—much to Guido's dismay.

Freud would have had a field day with these opposing scenarios. For him, detaching the libido from the deceased meant acknowledging what he called the "pastness" of a relationship that death has ended. He would have applauded Guido's capacity to recognize the finite, mortal nature of our earthly attractions and to stick his libido—re-aim that proverbial love gun—elsewhere. And he would have diagnosed Dante a terminal melancholic for being unable to get over Beatrice's death—for being someone who insisted on trying to love someone without a body. But it's difficult to psychoanalyze someone like Dante: Freudian terms like *libido* make little sense in situations that escape the barbed-wire fence of scientific explanation and spill into the dark wood of daydreams.

When Dante entered Mount Purgatory and saw Beatrice for the first time in *The Divine Comedy*, he was struggling to reconcile two different ideas of love. On the one hand, there was what he learned from Guido Cavalcanti—that love begins and ends with the body, and that love disappears when this body disappears from your life. On the other hand, there was Dante's own burgeoning sense that Beatrice's death was not the end of his love for her. That in fact her death was pushing him to come up with a whole new understanding of love itself—one that would separate him forever from Guido's teachings.

As Dante wrestled with these two conflicting notions of love, something unexpected happened. You could even call it miraculous. It turned out that *neither* approach to love could enable Dante to move beyond hell and purgatory and into paradise. There was a third option, and it wasn't about Beatrice per se. It was actually about Dante and the way that he had been dealing with Beatrice's death. In the *Vita Nuova*, her death was so mysterious and unfathomable that it compelled him to stop writing until he could gain a better understanding of it. Now, late in *Purgatorio*, over a decade after she died, he stood on the cusp of a powerful lesson, the one that had been missing in all the forlorn poetry of the *Vita Nuova*, and in all the self-pitying moments of *Inferno* and *Purgatorio*'s earlier cantos. It was ultimately a simple, even self-evident thing. But this lesson had to come from Beatrice, who would teach Dante that true love—the kind that outlives the mortal body—is fueled by faith and joy. Even in the face of death.

Love, faith, and joy. A new emotional Trinity. But to get to this lesson of Beatrice's, Dante had to take the biggest step of all, one that hadn't yet been asked of him in *Inferno* and *Purgatorio* despite their mighty challenges. To let love and faith and joy feed into one another Dante had to let go of nothing less than his former life, the person he had been till now.

You can't be reborn, Beatrice will teach Dante, unless you're willing to let a part of yourself die.

"SHE DIED CHOOSING MOTHERHOOD," THE head chaplain announced at the conclusion of the memorial service held at Bard for Katherine, just a week after her death.

An audience of about two hundred had filled the Chapel of the Holy Innocents, a beautiful, compact stone church at the center of campus. Its dark, cavernous vaults brimmed with the family I had grown up with, the friends I shared my life with, the mentors who had guided me, the colleagues I taught with, and the students I taught. I had chosen words from James Joyce's story "The Dead" for the program: *Why is it that words like these seem to me so dull and cold? Is it because there is no word tender enough to be your name?* But the words I heard were anything but dull and cold, as they tried to make sense of Katherine's life so that we could all come to terms with her death. A friend spoke of how Katherine had been a source of transparent joy and openheartedness in our guarded and cerebral academic world. He read a passage from Augustine's *Confessions*, when its broken author finally sees the blaze of God's light and feels its heat. The vocal arts students—the same ones whom I had been teaching that morning when the security guard came to my classroom to inform me of Katherine's accident—concluded the ceremony with a rendition of Aaron Copland's "At the River," a song that asks mourners to gather together by the waterside. As they sang, my students' faces were bathed in tears, their voices like those of the angels as they cut through the chapel's sobs and groans with radiant sound.

Days earlier, the head chaplain had come to the hospital to see me after the accident.

"Do you believe in the eternal life of the soul?" I asked him, just as I would ask my college president.

"I do," he said matter-of-factly, nodding his head.

He was a theologian who had spent his life studying religious books that he also believed in. I had spent my life studying *The Divine Comedy*, the story of how the soul becomes eternal. I felt Dante's words on intellectual and emotional levels, but his absolute faith in Christian doctrine belonged to an order of experience far removed from my secular world. I could think and feel with Dante in hell and purgatory—but I didn't know if I could believe with him in heaven.

The chaplain had spoken with Katherine briefly at a party the month before she died—the same party where she and I had met Astrid. The two beautiful pregnant women had stood together talking about children and the future, one with a world of sorrow behind her, having buried her husband, the other, filled with hopes and plans and innocent of what lay ahead. Katherine told the chaplain that evening that she had left acting to dedicate herself to our marriage, with dreams of raising our children. She had embraced her transition to wife and motherhood, the chaplain said, and she died having made it a reality. She died as the mother to her child.

She chose motherhood. Even before she actually became a mother, and even though she herself would never actually be a mother to her child (at least after the birth). But she had exercised Dante's treasured free will. In *The Divine Comedy*, it's not about how things actually turn out—it's about how you own a decision and a situation. In hell, the sinners like to think of themselves as victims of fate. In heaven, the blessed choose a path and are at peace with their decision, even if fate has something terrible and unexpected in store for them. Purgatory, the realm I now found myself in, was all about being able to evolve from the self-pity of hell to the free will of heaven.

Expelled from Florence, Dante needed a job and a place to live. He decided that he would offer his services as a court intellectual and diplomat to one of Italy's many independent city-states. To achieve this goal, he wrote a series of impressive books, which nowadays go by the pejorative tag *opere minori*, "minor works," because of the impossibly long shadows cast over them by *The Divine Comedy*: the *De vulgari eloquentia* (*On Eloquence in the Vernacular*, 1302–5), a history of the Romance languages and an impassioned plea for linguistic unity in fragmented Italy; and the *Convivio* (*Banquet*, 1304–7), a philosophical tome that tackles intellectual and theological concerns of the age.

As Dante wrote these learned tomes during those first years of exile, the lyric poetry and love stories that had inspired him to write the *Vita Nuova* seemed as remote to him as his lost homeland. He had gone from writing about the effects of passionate love to studying St. Thomas Aquinas's disquisition on the birth of the soul. When his ancestor Cacciaguida predicted Dante's exile in *Paradiso* 17, he might have put it like this, changing the last line of Dante's original tercet:

> *You will learn how salty is the taste*
> *of another man's bread, and how hard is the path*
> in a world without poetry.

Politics distracted Dante from poetry, then exile compelled him to devote his energies to rational thought, historical research, and speculative argument. He was brilliant enough to produce works of lasting value on all counts. The groundbreaking *De vulgari eloquentia* even earned Dante the epithet *padre della lingua italiana*, "father of the Italian language."

But there was a subject that neither the *De vulgari* nor the *Convivio* could handle: love, with all its mysteries. For that, only poetry would do. Exile had taken many things from him—but poetry was one thing that it could restore.

Poetry and life had always been inseparable for Dante. He chose to write *The Divine Comedy* in Tuscan rather than Latin, even though Latin, the universal language of the intellectual elite, would have initially guaranteed him many more readers. The Tuscan language was intelligible only to the small group connected to it by geography and local culture. But Dante knew that he could never capture the nuances of lived experience in a dead language—a living idiom was needed. That's where the poets come in. In *De vulgari*, Dante argues that poets are the guardians of language, responsible for transforming what is ephemeral and idiomatic into something universal. For good poets instinctively turn to what is lasting in everyday speech. They will opt for words in harmony with their Latin root while rejecting words containing what T.S. Eliot calls "local self-consciousness." "The Italian of Dante," Eliot writes, is "essentially the Italian of today." Dante, in Eliot's view, managed to write in a way that was accessible to many, without resorting to clichés and inert turns of phrase. His version of the everyday was utterly devoid of the commonplace. We see that drive for shared human experience as early as the opening lines of *The Divine Comedy*, with its talk of *nostra vita*, our life: "In the middle of *our life's* journey, / I found myself in a dark wood."

How did Dante realize that it was in the dark wood of poetry that his writing belonged, and that projects like the *De vulgari eloquentia* and *Convivio* were not his life's calling? Something was pulling him to his old obsessions, Beatrice and poetry, which had always been one and the same. Perhaps deep down, Dante understood it was time to say good-bye to what he describes as the evil and impious company that he conspired with early in his exile. When he accepted that he would never return to Florence, he figured that he did not have to keep writing the books that other people wanted; he would write the books—the *book*, actually—that he alone believed in. And in so doing he would fulfill the promise that he had made at the end of the *Vita Nuova*: to write books tender enough to be worthy of Beatrice's name.

A YEAR OUT OF GRADUATE school in 2001, I spent the day at the Columbia University library chasing down footnotes and verifying sources for a scholarly article on Voltaire's reading of Dante. This meant agonizing over such issues as whether to cite an ellipsis with or without brackets, capitalize foreign titles, and modernize ancient spellings.

"Not a bad day's work, is it?" I said later that evening over dinner in the East Village to a woman I was trying to impress.

She shot me a withering look.

But it didn't bother me. My article continued the happy years of solitary confinement that I had spent in graduate school, locked inside a study carrel in Yale's Sterling Library, surrounded by studies of Dante's reception and the marbled covers of Voltaire's *oeuvres complètes*. It was old, musty stuff, but it verified my authenticity as a real scholar. I could tell you why Goethe thought Dante's idea of justice was barbaric, and why Victor Hugo liked to stare at *Inferno*'s fire but couldn't adjust his eyes to *Paradiso*'s light. I was well on my way to becoming an expert on how people read *The Divine Comedy* centuries after it had been written—soon I would rule supreme over my own little academic duchy.

My research at Columbia that day would culminate in *Romantic Europe and the Ghost of Italy* in 2008, the scholarly book whose proof pages I labored over in a Westerly apartment during the first months after Katherine's death. Editing this book had given me peace and quiet in the Underworld, and when the book finally appeared I had finished my season in hell and was in purgatory. The dedication to that book reads:

In loving memory of my wife
Katherine Lynne Mester
1970–2007
And for our daughter
Isabel Katherine Luzzi

I had been tempted to put Isabel's dates below her name, *2007–*, to show the symmetry of Katherine's life in Isabel. But I thought better of it, not wanting to slap something so monumental, so portentous, on my baby girl.

That open-ended date applied to me as well as Isabel. What would I do after 2007, I wondered, without Katherine? The idea of writing another learned tome that exhausted the nonscholarly at a glance exhausted me as well. In Saul Bellow's *Ravelstein*, the narrator, Chick, checks out the work of a supposedly brilliant scholar, only to find that reading it makes him feel like an ant trying to cross the Andes. Around this time I was granted tenure, a lifetime guarantee of employment. I could go on producing more road maps to the Andes for tiny feet, and would even be rewarded for doing so. This would mean staying on the path of Guido Cavalcanti, for whom work (poetry) was a rarefied pursuit not meant for the common (the *volgare*). Or I could follow Dante, who dared to change his writing style as he changed his definition of living and loving.

Would I find the courage to write about love's mysteries, I wondered as I attached the dedication to an email for my publisher, or would I continue to probe the joys and sorrows of Voltaire's library?

LADY, WHY DO YOU SHAME him so?

The angels in the Earthly Paradise atop Mount Purgatory ask Beatrice this question when she scolds Dante, just moments after Virgil has left. Beatrice is quick to answer: this man, Dante, had marvelous potential for good, but then instead of blossoming his soul went to seed:

> *For a time my face sustained him:*
> *showing him my youthful eyes,*
> *I led him with me on the right path.*

Up until this point in the poem there has been an unspoken but palpable aspect of Dante's personality, a feeling that has comforted him, but also held him back: his self-pity. Over losing Florence. Entering the dark wood. Saying good-bye to Beatrice. He has every right to his self-pity—or, to use a Freudian term, his melancholy. He had loved Beatrice, loved Florence, loved his former life, and lost them all. But Beatrice knows he can do better. He needs to return to poetry and the mysteries of love, the project that he started in the *Vita Nuova*. So she asks three monumental things of him:

Change his definition of love—which will mean his definition of her.

Change his definition of poetry—which will transform how he writes about her.

And say good-bye to his former life—which will mean saying good-bye to the person he once was and everyone attached to it, especially Guido.

As difficult as this task is, Beatrice has simplified it. All that Dante has to do is agree to her charges, sign the contract; she'll prepare the draft by rewriting Dante's first book, the *Vita Nuova*, right before his ears and eyes at the end of *Purgatory*.

IN MY SECOND YEAR OF graduate school, long after I had abandoned the dream of becoming a writer and embraced the academic life, I traveled to Calabria to visit relatives and my family's ancestral home. I had taken the trip often since college and had become good friends with my cousin Giuseppe. During my time in southern Italy, his parents—my aunt Filomena and uncle Giorgio, the man whose verbatim recitation of Ugolino's words had first set my love for Dante in motion— treated me like a son. Everyone made a big fuss when I showed up, the (relatively speaking) tall, educated, fancy-pants cousin from *l'America*, with his alligator shirts and bag of paperbacks. They called me *u professoru* in the dialect and ribbed me about my bookworm ways, but they seemed to relish my visits. They filled me with homemade pasta and carafes of wine and entertained me with long rides into the Sila, the ancient mountain forest atop Cosenza, the province where my family had lived for centuries.

On this visit Giuseppe took me to the stone hut that my mother, father, and four siblings had inhabited before immigrating to the United States. We stopped by a nearby house and knocked on the door. A squat, grimacing man, apparently the proprietor, emerged. Giuseppe knew him and explained that I, *figlio di Pasquale e Yolanda Luzzi*, had come to see the land and house that had once belonged to his parents. Indeed, the land and house may technically still have belonged to them. The man, who apparently had taken control of the property by squatting on it, looked daggers at me. The old Casa Luzzi may have been the occasion for a sentimental act of tourism for me, but for him it was a matter of life and death. Giuseppe insisted we were only visiting.

"Vo' giust' vedere 'a terra dei suoi antenati," Giuseppe said. "He just wants to see the land of his people."

Threatening me with his stare, the man let us pass.

Nature had reclaimed the house. A voracious group of weeds surrounded the perimeter and penetrated the cracks in the walls. I was careful not to cut myself on the thorns as I approached the front door and tried to peer in through the broken glass. Inside it was dark so I could make out very little. But even in the bad light I could see that my family had lived in the most spartan conditions. There were dirt floors and no bathroom—the house seemed to sprout like a weed out of the dusty hillside. There was no separation between nature and home, the opposite of what I had known in Rhode Island in our comfortable house on a tree-lined street. My family had left the Calabrian dust in 1956 to come to America, and now, a generation later, I returned to discover our origins. I knew I had to tell this story, and on some unconscious level I must have sworn to myself that I would not go back to Calabria until I did.

But I wasn't ready. I had hard work to do in graduate school, and it was no time for other dreams. *Just hold on to this story,* I told myself as Giuseppe and I stood among the brambles, *don't lose it.* I had said good-bye to Tristan and Iseult, which had meant good-bye to storytelling—at least for a while.

Later that sun-soaked evening, Giuseppe and I sat in his garden talking about what it would have been like if my family had remained in Calabria—or if he had followed the Luzzi herd to America. As a young man, he had been promised to my cousin Margaret, née Immacolata Luzzi, before she emigrated from Calabria to the U.S. They both ended up marrying someone else.

"*Com'era bella!*" Giuseppe exclaimed, "How beautiful she was!" Then he pulled out his guitar, and I recorded him singing the famous (and famously cheesy) pop song by Toto Cutugno:

Lasciatemi cantare
con la chitarra in mano . . .
sono un italiano
un italiano vero.

Let me sing
with a guitar in my hand . . .
I'm an Italian
a true Italian.

By then Giuseppe believed that my work would bring me back to Calabria for much more wine and many more songs together. But that would be my last trip. It wasn't just the inconveniences that kept me away. Yes, the train south from Florence was slow, Giorgio and Filomena's house tiny and uncomfortable (especially the outdoor bathroom with its arctic trickle of a shower), and the Calabrians I wasn't related to were suspicious and unwelcoming. But in truth I stayed away—with excuses to Giuseppe like, "*Sai, con l'insegnamento e le ricerche, il viaggio è difficile . . .*" ("You know, with teaching and research, the trip is difficult . . .")—because the visit to my family's stone hut had brought my time in Calabria full circle. I felt like I no longer needed to spend time there as a visitor and tourist, and I wished instead to give a new life to the story of my family's homeland. I wanted to put this story into words.

So I never heard Giuseppe sing that song again, about the true Italian and the guitar he couldn't let go of.

OUR LIVES ARE DEFINED IN single moments, buoyed by powers beyond our control—as pleased another, Dante's Ulysses would say. But there are things we can control, even amid the searing challenges of a tragic *vita nuova*. After years of fearing and doing legal battle with Eddie Knight, I had forgiven him, which helped me finally rid myself of paralyzing hatred and self-pity. Beatrice understands that sometimes we are incapable of taking fate into our own hands. So, after scolding Dante in Mount Purgatory, she gives him a simple command:

Say, say if this is true. To this accusation
your confession must be joined.

Dante has only to open his mouth and say *yes*—just a single word that will enable him to move out of the purgatory of self-pity and into the heaven of free will. It should be the easiest thing he's ever done, but that single syllable of affirmation at first won't come out. Wild emotions struggle within Dante—then they send forth a sound from his mouth:

> *Confusion and fear combined*
> *to drive a "yes" from my mouth—*
> *but you needed eyes to hear it.*

With this exhale of free will, Dante says good-bye to his youthful love for Beatrice, his youthful definition of poetry, and what is more, his crushing self-pity. Now everything is possible. Especially love and poetry.

A FEW WEEKS BEFORE KATHERINE died, she and I were lying in bed together, and she told me a story about a person who, in her words, "never showed any kindness." The way she told the story—without guile or judgment or rancor—made me think: *thank God I didn't marry someone like me, an over-thinker!* I would have turned the situation around and around, seeking to cast blame, finding my own righteous place in the story. While Katherine simply made it into a tale of how one should and should not act. She had lived in New York for over a decade, yet she was as fresh as though she had arrived in town only yesterday after saying good-bye to her tight-knit Midwestern family in a rickety train depot. I spent my days thinking about ancient stories, about why Dante and Guido fell out and the changing nature of Dante's love for Beatrice.

Katherine lived in the here and now; I lived in the far away and long before.

At the beginning of our relationship, and in my vanity, I believed that I had much to teach her. In truth it was I who would become the student and she the *professoressa*. With Katherine, I was learning that I didn't have to dream of a better life or try to write myself into one—I already had one with her.

On Friday nights we would go to a Thai restaurant in Catskill, a sad rundown town not far from Bard. Inside the restaurant, local families sat on plastic chairs alongside walls festooned with T-shirts and other cheap decorations. The owner of the restaurant, a pasty guy from Queens, took our order while his pretty, heavyset Thai wife prepared the meals. It was our oasis. We never ran into other Bard people there, and it was not the place where vacationing New Yorkers popped in. It was a place I could relax in and be a *Luzzi*-rhymes-with-*fuzzy*. The steaming plates bathed in peanut curry would arrive, and from their first mouthwatering dollop onto my tongue, I felt like I had returned to my first and most familiar metaphysical village, its red tomato sauces given an equally delicious Asian inflection.

No relationship can be all things. Ours was not about exchanging ideas and bringing my life as a teacher and a scholar into our home. Katherine was a willing listener when I told her about whatever I happened to be working on, but she didn't push me to sharpen or rethink my intellectual principles. I talked about my scholarship with her the way that one talks about one's job to someone in a different line: in general terms and in the form of a progress report. I could not ask her advice on how to shape an argument or construe a writer. That was my responsibility, one I thrilled to, and something that I left at the office at the end of the day. I had no need to tell stories: I was living one.

After her death, the old ambitions, the old restlessness started to resurface. Part of it had to do with wanting to make the most of what I now knew was the fragility of my time on earth, what Virgil called the temporal fire. But there was a more private, deeply felt reason. With Katherine, I had considered becoming an academic administrator because the money would help us while channeling my ambitions in a worthy and stimulating direction; without her, I set my sight on something closer to my heart, a target at once higher yet less clearly marked. Losing Katherine took me back to my old desire to reach readers outside the ivory tower. I used to dream of publishing in learned journals, but once I achieved this, I realized how few people actually read them. And when *Romantic Europe and the Ghost of Italy* appeared, my sisters all proudly bought it and gamely tried to read it. But after a few pages, they felt like Bellow's ant trying to cross the Andes. My book became a mantelpiece decoration. An object, in my mother's words, of *bellamente*, beautification—something to behold, not experience.

There has to be another way to write, I told myself. I never once doubted the worthiness of that first book whose page proofs had sustained me in the Underworld. But I believed I had another voice, one that didn't speak in fancy academic phrases—one that had tried to tell of Tristan and Iseult. *Live a life of meaning.* The phrase played over and over as I grieved and then mourned Katherine, and as I continued to study the person and the poem that had provided a road map out of hell and purgatory. I could never hope to write like Dante, but his lessons were available to all. Deep into his exile, he had found the courage to leave the safety of the scholar's world and return to his first passion, poetry, and all the promise it held for answering his lifelong obsession with the question, *What is love?* Death had brought into focus something that I could no longer deny: a life of meaning would mean a life of writing.

On the endless commutes between Tivoli and Westerly, I told myself stories to pass the time as I drove along the spine of Connecticut on Route 84. I silently narrated the tale of my family's Calabrian stone hut, replaying the notes streaming from my cousin Giuseppe's guitar as he dreamed of his lost love Immacolata. Those sad hours of travel were my motorized version of the purgatorial climb. From Danbury to Southbury to Waterbury, I composed my first pages since Paris that didn't involve parsing someone else's ideas. Then, after three and a half hours on the road, I would exit Connecticut and enter Rhode Island, where the cast of characters of my strange *vita nuova* was waiting. Then it would be time to cut my stories short and file them away for the return commute to Bard a few days later.

There was no question at that point of writing these stories down and translating my daydreams into drafts—I still had no one to show them to.

Or so I thought. In truth, I had been showing my stories to Dante all along, and I had been writing all along, just in a different key that I knew must now change. My early ambition, like Dante's, had been to gain acceptance in a prestigious world that would mark a distance between where I came from and my career aspirations. For me, that meant climbing the ladder of the ivory tower, out of my Calabrian immigrant roots; for Dante, it had meant earning the respect of Guido Cavalcanti and the other Sweet New Style poets who welcomed him into their charmed circle. Tragedy had taught Dante—and it had taught me—that an elite life is not enough, that to make use of any gift you need to leave your comfort zone and do work that you truly believe in. Exile pulled Dante away from rarefied lyrics and abstract philosophy and into the universal voice that made *The Divine Comedy* so gripping and extraordinary for the common reader. For me, Katherine's death shattered the self-contained world where I wrote scholarship for the tiniest slice of readers, and drew me back toward the kind of writing that had first inspired me: the storytelling that led me to write of Tristan and Iseult. Beatrice and Virgil taught Dante that what is important is not the act but the decision behind it—the free will that makes you fully inhabit your life's choices. Learning to love Katherine in her absence had taught me that I could no longer pretend to be someone I was not, and that storytelling had always been my life's chosen path. I now needed to muster the courage to accept it, and live accordingly.

I am no modern-day Dante; but studying him had enabled me to climb out of my grief and mourning and find something magical that these electric states had left behind. That is the real magical thinking of grief. That other life that death throws you into—the one that you wanted nothing to do with—is actually one you can build upon. For it contains the gifts that the person you loved left behind for you.

The commute from Bard to Westerly was a soul-crunching one, and I took it two times a week for three years. I stopped at the exact halfway point each trip, a Dunkin' Donuts in Southbury, Connecticut, where I would use the bathroom and buy a coffee and a bagel. On my way out of the parking lot, I would pass a Subway, its plastic awning reminding me of the one I would pass in Westerly at the other extreme of my exile's life. It was strip mall country, just like the louche commercial developments I had grown up with. But I didn't have to accept the ugliness of my surroundings, nor the monotony of the commute. For I was writing now, in my head and on the move, and I could do it anywhere. There was no need to move to Paris and rent a garret.

Long study and great love—Dante's words to Virgil on how a lifetime of immersing himself in the *Aeneid* had taught him how to become not just a writer, but the kind of writer that best expressed his free will. The legend about Dante staring at Florence from the hills of San Miniato had it all wrong: it wasn't just that Dante was reaching back toward Florence in those first years of exile, it was that he was reaching away from it as well, searching for a new life that he had not yet decided upon or made his own. He was still wandering around Tuscany on the outskirts of Florence, trying to get back to his former life; he was writing, but not yet writing what he knew deep down to be his life's work. Because in those first years the paralysis of self-pity was keeping Dante from embracing his free will. Had he stared from San Miniato to the Baptistery of San Giovanni in the center of Florence where he had been baptized, and to Giotto's Campanile towering alongside it, Dante would also have been staring deep inside himself, where poetry lived waiting for him to embrace it.

The coffee and bagel from Dunkin' Donuts in Southbury made the final hour and a half pass quickly, as did the thought of seeing Isabel. The cascading words I composed behind the steering wheel were a feast of memory that would become the first book of my *vita nuova*. When I finally sat down to write this book in 2011, the year my commutes to Rhode Island ended, the hard part of composing the work in my imagination had been done. I used to daydream about Giuseppe and his guitar playing in Calabria, wondering when I would ever write about them. On those lonely commutes, sanctioned by Dante's example and his teaching, I had embraced the idea that I would tell Giuseppe's and my family's story, which became my first book written for general readers, *My Two Italies*. What is more, my decision to write this book—a quiet act of free will as simple as Dante's *yes* to Beatrice at the end of *Purgatorio*—gave me the strength finally to build a life for myself beyond the Underworld.

NOR WOULD THE STORY END with *My Two Italies*. That faraway day I spent an hour with the angels by Katherine's grave in the Detroit suburbs, I was given a glimpse of something terrible and profound, unspeakably private and yet also something that I could put into words, and not only for myself. *Why share?* I wondered after her service at Royal Oak Cemetery, where Katherine's family and I had watched her coffin lowered into the ground. We had driven to the spot in a long black hearse, and on that secluded winding path I felt as though we had exited planet earth to arrive at a place of utter tranquility, a sparse green field buffered by soaring pines. In the years that would follow, as that exhortation *live a life of meaning* goaded me on, I came to understand that I was being asked back to that spot in Royal Oak, to describe what it was like to find yourself suddenly in the Underworld. Early in *Inferno*, as he is racked with fear, Dante says to Virgil, *Why me? I'm no Aeneas, no Saint Paul*, heroes who had been to hell and back. Like Dante, for years I was paralyzed by the fear of going back to hell and resuming my conversations with the dead. Katherine's tomb never offered me any solace, just as I imagine that Dante's alleged view of Florence from the hills of San Miniato never comforted him. I cannot know what went through Dante's mind in those first bitter years of exile, but I believe that it was only when he decided to write about the life he had lost that he was able to stop staring at it, just as I was only able to open myself again to love when I began to write about the pain of losing it.

III

One Thousand and One

E QUINDI USCIMMO A RIVEDER LE STELLE.
AND THEN WE EMERGED TO SEE THE STARS AGAIN.

III

CHAPTER 7

Posthoc7

ante enters *Paradiso*, the last canticle of *The Divine Comedy*, to find a flood of light:

> The glory of Him who moves all things
> suffuses the universe, and shines
> in one part more and elsewhere less.

Most readers fail to appreciate this luminous spectacle, preferring the flames of hell and the slopes of purgatory. The French writer Victor Hugo even claimed that in *Paradiso*, "we don't see ourselves anymore . . . the human eye was not made to look upon so much light, and when the poem becomes happy, it becomes boring."

Paradiso is indeed challenging. Gone are the tortured souls and winding confessions of Francesca da Rimini and Ulysses. Gone too is the expert guidance of Virgil. Dante himself barely made it into heaven. It took Beatrice's ferocious rebuke atop Mount Purgatory to get him to stop feeling sorry for himself and take responsibility for his past. Only a woman's love could get him into heaven, and only a woman's love could guide him through it—she will be with him every step of the way. Hugo got it wrong: Dante's poem doesn't become boring when it becomes happy. It's just hard to get rid of the things that stand in the way of happiness. But once you do—as Dante was able to, thanks to Beatrice's firm but loving guidance—the light can be spectacular.

Paradiso has a particularly medieval happy ending—that's why Dante called his very unfunny poem a *commedia*, following Aristotle's definition of comedy as a work that ends well. Before its blissful conclusion, *The Divine Comedy* charts the endless heartache of souls who burn with love: the most memorable characters in the poem are the damned, not the saved. From a young age, Dante hobnobbed with the upper echelons of culture and power, from his time as a poet in the Sweet New Style to his election as one of Florence's leading politicians. In exile, he continued to orbit lofty spheres as a diplomat and court intellectual. But worldly success cannot heal a broken heart, and Dante proves no exception to this unwritten rule of human experience. He identified most with those who, like him, found themselves on the wrong side of fate. Who looks after the world's victims, his poem asks; who shares in the world's sorrows? To get to the ultimate joy in *Paradiso*, Dante needed someone to absorb his pain. This person couldn't be Beatrice—she was too much a part of the joy to attend to his sorrow. It had to be someone whose business was pain and heartache—someone for whom suffering was life's chosen path.

Absorb our pain. This is what a mother does. Someone who nurtures and protects us when we can't do so ourselves. For the Christian Dante, the role fell to Christ's mother, the Virgin Mary.

In *Paradiso* 33, Dante looks around for Beatrice as he enters the upper reaches of heaven, but she isn't there. Instead, there is a different woman beside him. Dante's eyes become an ocean of celestial light and the sight of her is blinding. He bows his head in front of the Virgin Mary, for humility is the only suitable response to the kaleidoscope of love and sorrow that she embodies.

> *Love was relit in your womb,*
> *whose warmth has brought this flower*
> *to bloom in eternal peace.*

That's right, Dante must have thought: *when the world around you crumbles, you turn to the person whose womb first lit the world with love.*

ABSORB OUR PAIN.

For Isabel and me, there was one person who best understood this language of love and sorrow.

On December 23, 2007, the day I first brought Isabel to Rhode Island from Tivoli, I struggled to install her car seat. I have never been mechanically adept, so this was no surprise. Still in my initial shock over Katherine's death, I found anything associated with taking care of Isabel overwhelming, even something as basic as ensuring her safety in the car. So I actually called the local police and asked for their expert on car seat installation—there is such a person. Within minutes, a large, unfriendly blond cop showed up at my door, looking ominously like the Czech guard who had forced me to detrain at Dresden when I showed up without a visa. With no humor and exaggerated seriousness, he rattled off all the reasons why my seat was ill suited for peanut-sized Isabel, and then he proceeded to strap her in so tightly that she could barely breathe. Afterward, as he idled his car in the parking lot, he seemed to hesitate about whether he should call in my case and make sure I didn't travel with Isabel. He finally drove off fifteen minutes later, leaving us free to travel. The car bursting with luggage, sheets, books, food, and clothes, we eased onto Route 9G, the same road that Katherine had driven her last morning on earth. I sat in the front alone, with Isabel strapped in the back.

But there was someone else in the car with my daughter and me, the person who had replaced my late wife as Isabel's main caregiver: my mother sat next to Isabel in the backseat, where she could keep her eyes on my infant daughter. My mother had raised my five siblings and me by appealing only to her own intuitions and the knowledge that she had inherited from centuries of her southern Italian culture. She applied this nononsense nurturing to establish domestic order in Isabel's and my home, as our small family reeled from sudden death. As we drove from Tivoli to Westerly, my mom held Isabel's hand, singing to her in a Calabrian dialect that I could barely understand.

Chi è 'sa piccerella, 'sa piccerella bella?

Who is this little girl, this beautiful little girl?

YOLANDA LUZZI HAD BEEN PREPARING for this car ride since childhood. Her life of care began when she was a young girl growing up in Calabria, the poor mountainous region in southern Italy where her adopted brother, my uncle Giorgio, had declaimed Dante's verses about the cannibalistic Count Ugolino by heart. At the start of each day, she gathered eggs from the chickens and tended to the other small animals on her family farm, and then she followed her mother around the house from one chore to the next. Her father, Carmine Crocco, owned a bit of land, so there was always plenty of work, from cooking and cleaning to babysitting and gardening. Yolanda quickly became a master of all things domestic. In a harsh landscape and among a fatalistic people, my mother had an unusually comfortable life. "There was fruit, meat, cheese," she always said. "We lacked for nothing."

One day a handsome and powerfully built Calabrian man from down-mountain—Yolanda's home was higher up the slope—caught sight of her and her family's land. He fell in love with both on the spot. Pasquale Luzzi had just returned to Calabria after three years in Germany, first as a military internee of the Nazis after Italy had left the Axis in 1943, then as the husband of the Bavarian woman with whom he had started an affair while working as an enforced laborer on her family farm, the threat of death shadowing his every embrace with the blond enemy. His family back in his village thought he had died in the war—and he had indeed been slated for execution for disobeying a German soldier by refusing to dig a ditch one day, just barely escaping death thanks to the wildly unanticipated intervention of a German officer. But he had managed to flee from Germany and was now back in his hometown. As with Beatrice for Dante, one look was all it took for Pasquale: Yolanda Crocco would be his. My father was not a man you said no to—and so on August 17, 1948, Yolanda and Pasquale Luzzi were married before the eyes of God and the newly reconstituted Italian Republic. She was four months shy of her fifteenth birthday.

By sixteen she was pregnant, and, after an initial miscarriage, at age seventeen she gave birth to her first child, a son named Angelo, the first of six children. Her life of domestic service had officially begun. She never worked outside of the home or learned to drive. Her day started before dawn, when she would wake with Pasquale at three thirty a.m. to get him ready for work. After the family immigrated to the U.S. in 1956, this meant laying out his clothes and preparing an enormous amount of food to fuel him through his long shifts as a machinist and then outdoor landscaper. She packed sandwiches of pepper and egg, wedges of soppressata, and slabs of bread and cheese along with a thermos of black coffee in his industrial-scale black lunchbox. When he left the house at four a.m., she returned to her spot on the sofa—she slept separately from the hard-snoring Pasquale—and dozed in and out of sleep for a few hours until her children woke up. Then it was round two of prep: a mortadella and provolone sandwich on a homemade roll along with homemade wine-biscuit cookies for my lunch, an ironed shirt and pants for my brother, pressed dresses for my sisters, and breakfast for us all.

The tiny upstairs of our home was a train station of coming-and-going siblings. When I was in grade school I would awake at eight and find my sister Rose, twelve years my senior, making up her face in front of the bathroom mirror, her wet hair wrapped into a turban-shaped towel as she listened to the Andrews Sisters sing "Rum and Coca-Cola" or "Bei Mir Bist Du Schön." Meanwhile, my other older sister Mary finished sipping her coffee before scurrying out the door to Walgreen's where she worked as a cashier. By this time, the oldest daughter, Margaret, had married and moved two streets away, so we were five kids at home, including my brother Angelo, eighteen years older than me and keeper of strange hours. While I wolfed down bowls of Froot Loops across the table from my complaining younger sister, Tina—"Ma, please tell Joey to shut his mouth when he eats, it's disgusting!"—Angelo would be sleeping off a night of poker on the downstairs sofa in a refurbished basement coated with cooking grease. My siblings and I were like the disjointed hands of a large Calabrian clock, moving in disparate time throughout the day, all of our schedules and movements synchronized by our mother, who set everything in motion and oiled any jammed gears.

Come dinnertime, I would sit down to the table alone, and my mother would serve me something lavish like my favorite meal: steak, corn, and mashed potatoes, with a pool hollowed out in the billowy starch for cooking oil that I would soak up with slabs of her bread. I ate after sports practice ended at six p.m.—after my father and his massive five p.m. meal, a conflagration of pasta sauces, stewed meats, bottles of wine, and pickled vegetables consumed in a haze of Marlboro Red cigarette smoke. My sisters never seemed to sit down for food: for them, it was a rice cake here, a bowl of soup there, the occasional sandwich of fresh bread lathered with mayonnaise and filled with the soft flesh of one of our garden-grown tomatoes. My brother was never around for dinner, either: he liked to have his heaping dish of pasta on the Old Country schedule, at noon. Juggling her steaming platters to keep all these various bellies full, my mother never sat: she carted plates from one sitting to the next, filling and refilling the pots and pans with ingredients and oil, occasionally taking a break to gobble some sauce-free pasta or unbuttered bread in between her mad sprints from stove to table. After all the meals were eaten, there was cleanup. After cleanup, there was my father and then my younger sister and me to get ready for bed while she monitored the whereabouts of my older siblings, making sure my brother had a snack before heading out to the social club, and warning my sisters to come home early—and alone—if they had a date. On a good night, she would enjoy a half hour of television as a reward. She loved the sitcoms, from the intricate plots of *All in the Family* to the double entendres of *Two and a Half Men*. She would laugh to lines that she didn't understand, the studio audience's good cheer enough to delight her. But if anyone walked in the room she would hand them the remote and say, *"Tiena, guarda chilla che ti para, io zigno stuffa di 'sa merda"*—"Here, watch what you want, I'm tired of this shit." At ten o'clock, after the rest of us, except my brother—still out playing cards at his club—had gone to bed, my mother fluffed the pillows on her pullout sofa for some sleep. Perhaps it was because the day kept racing around her head, or maybe it was the prospect of the upcoming tasks looming hours away—but, for whatever reason, true rest was elusive, and she would spend most of the night tossing and turning before hearing my father's familiar rumble down the hallway at three thirty a.m.

By 2007, these routines of my mother's were only memories.

After my father died in 1995, my mother began to wear a black dress of mourning and she would not take it off for two years. It got to the point where I couldn't imagine her in a world of color, as she and everything around her had faded into half-tones and gray scale, and what had been her formidable energy had disappeared along with her green print dresses and blue floral scarves. She still didn't sleep, and still had no interests outside of her house and her family. But the center of her world had shifted: with my father no longer there to boss her around and provide her with a million and one to-dos, she suddenly had something that she had never known: free time. At first she was at a loss as to how to handle it.

Then, slowly, her life began to take a new shape. Though she was wide awake most of the night, she found that she could blissfully doze off between six and eight a.m., a period of high-octane activity while my father was alive. She also started to inhabit what had been the forbidden city of my childhood: upstairs, the nicer part of the house, with attractive and comfortable sofas and a large television, a space that my father had jealously cordoned off, as though it were a precious metal that would drop in value if tarnished by anyone else's human touch. She had her coffee upstairs each morning, watched television there at night, and even invited her friends to visit. Finally, for the first time in fifty years, she had peace and quiet and time to think. She no longer had to surrender the remote during *Everybody Loves Raymond*.

The day after we arrived in Rhode Island from Tivoli, I found my mother crying in anguish in the kitchen, asking God why he had inflicted so much pain and suffering on her. She had spent fifty turbulent years with a loving but domineering husband who ruled our home with an iron fist, making sure we kept the heating and lighting at a bare minimum even in the cold and dark New England winters. My father was no different from his Calabrian brothers in his steroidal patriarchy, and within this archaic domestic structure my mother took enormous pride in making our home a beautifully ordered space that fostered the tightest of family bonds. We may not have eaten together, but my siblings and I were intensely connected, as I came to see in them a set of junior parents who helped me with my "American" responsibilities—homework, filling out school forms, making sure I had the right sports equipment—while my mother and father provided the raw essentials of food, shelter, and fiercely protective love. Despite his obsessive need to control things, my father realized how blessed he was to have someone like Yolanda, whom he openly praised and cherished, especially after his stroke at age fifty-nine, which made him entirely dependent on her care for the last thirteen years of his life.

My mother knew she had accomplished an enormous amount in the new world—but still, the journey from Calabria to Rhode Island had been a dramatic, difficult one: she had abandoned her homeland for an American culture whose permissive morals she would never understand; she had seen two of her children divorce; and now she was living through the horrific death of a young woman whom she had adored, the wife of her son and mother of her now motherless grand-daughter. Her tears in the kitchen that day were tears of anger and frustration, but not of self-pity—she did not need a Beatrice to teach her not to feel sorry for herself. She had never cultivated her own interests or followed her own pursuits. She had given her life to her husband and children, and while it was not an easy life for her, she had fully embraced her role as nurturer and caregiver, fulfilling her life's purpose. She stood at the center of a large and devoted family that adored her—so much that, within ten years of my father's death, all of my siblings except for me had remained within her orbit. For my mom, life was not about acquiring things or discovering her interests and passions; it was about the lives that she created and then cared for. The day she moved in with me and Isabel in Tivoli, her luggage consisted of some underwear, a few simple tops and stretch pants, a pair of patent leather shoes, and a black duffel jacket from JCPenney. In a ziplock plastic bag were her false teeth and toothbrush. My sister Rose later told me, "That night in the hospital, after we all found out about Katherine, she knew what she had to do." Indeed, my mother shed few tears the day Katherine died— they would come later. Instead, she sat still and stoic, already imagining the duties of a motherhood that she had long since abandoned. I never had to ask for her help.

Yolanda Luzzi had at least one more act to go in her life as a mother, and she was as prepared as she'd ever been. When she saw me come into the kitchen that day I found her weeping, she quietly pulled her face up from her hands and rubbed her eyes dry, before asking me if I'd like a cup of coffee.

DANTE BEGINS THE NINETY-NINTH OF his one hundred cantos with a prayer to the Virgin Mary, whom he describes as "more humble and exalted than any other creature." Despite the beauty of these words, I never understood why Dante devoted the choicest real estate of his poem—where he is about to complete his journey through Paradiso and come face-to-face with God—to an impossibly pure woman who had not played a large role in his poem till then. I wondered if Dante was just acting the part of the dutiful Christian, with a Hail Mary crafted to order. But this was before I watched my nearly eighty-year-old mother, plagued by insomnia, rheumatism, arthritis, and tinnitus, give up a hard-won, peaceful life near her family and friends to help me raise my daughter far from her home.

For three years, Yolanda Luzzi lived out of that suitcase and collection of plastic bags as she bounced back and forth without complaint between my apartment in Tivoli and her home in Westerly. She asked for nothing from me and bore her self-appointed responsibility with grace and silence. I wasn't particularly good company. Every time I looked at her lined face and false teeth, every time I heard her broken English or ungrammatical Italian, I was forced to accept that I shared a roof with my mother instead of my young and beautiful wife. She took my sullenness for what it was—a selfish and unwitting refusal to move forward.

But it wasn't in her to judge, only to care for me and for Isabel. For the most part, she stayed out of my hair and let me do what I wanted—unless it affected Isabel. Only once did she chime in on my affairs, and that was when things were heating up with Astrid. She saw that I was in over my head with this cool customer of a German, grasping for a life that wasn't true to what Astrid wanted, or to what Isabel and I needed.

"*Ti ho lasciato in pace finora*," she said to me the night after I returned from Christmas with Astrid in Germany, "*ma chista volta te lo dico buono: chilla donna non sarà mai 'na matra per tua figlia*"— "I've left you in peace till now, but this time I'm going to tell you straight-up: that woman will never be a mother to your child."

Yolanda was not a woman prone to grand pronouncements. I wanted to argue with her, to tell her she was wrong, that she didn't understand. But I knew better than to ask her not to peer into the soul of her flesh and blood and see my wounded desire. She knew only to speak the truth—and so I listened.

When Dante reaches out to Mary, he asks her for three things: kindness, clemency, and compassion: to be nurtured, to be forgiven, and for her to share his pain. Mary had no earthly power. She did not make the heavens and the nations and the seas. She was only the humble girl who consecrated her existence to the divine child that she carried, gave birth to, and raised only to watch him die. Her life was one of sacrifice, and her blessing was the one that, except for God's, Dante sought beyond all others.

I didn't need to ask for the blessings that Yolanda Luzzi shed over Isabel and me like falling autumn leaves—the image chosen by Virgil and Dante to describe the souls bunched together on the shores of the Underworld, a picture of relentless despair that my mother strained to infuse with hope.

IN JUNE 2010, THREE YEARS into my hometown exile, I bought a modest house in Tivoli, a few hundred yards from the apartment where Katherine and I had lived. Finally, I thought as I signed the papers and forked over the deposit, I was escaping the endless fallout from her death and making a new start. Finally, I would be living with Isabel. She would be enrolled in the pre-K program at Bard, where she could play with the children of my friends, and the exhausting commutes from Tivoli to Westerly would be over. When I was in Westerly those three years, I used to go to parent activities with Isabel at the Mystic Aquarium where Isabel would learn about crustaceans and anemones. The young mothers just looked through me. They were all married with one child on hand and others on the way, and I was the outsider, an older parent with no wedding ring and no visible connection to their community. The house in Tivoli would reconnect me to the living.

There was only one problem, however, and, to quote Astrid once more, it was a big one. The same problem that had caused my Rhode Island exile in the first place: my persistent inability to strike out on my own with Isabel. On September 5, 2010, Isabel and I officially moved into our new home. On the drive from Westerly to Tivoli, my mom was seated in the back of the car just as she had been on that first drive to Westerly three years earlier. I had made it out of the electric air of grief and was working my way through the uphill slog of mourning, and at each stage my mother was there to help me—a maternal version of Virgil, offering her profound wisdom on children and family life at a time when I desperately needed a guide to both.

The gay marriage movement was then in full swing, and what had been the typical American family was morphing at the speed of light. In our progressive college town, it was not unusual to see children brought to school by two men, or two women, a single mom, or a single dad—and, in our case, a widowed man and his widowed mother. In fact, the parents, teachers, and care providers at Isabel's pre-K, who had long been waiting for me to return with Isabel to the Bard community, embraced us. They even started to call my mother Nonnie, as she became the school's adopted grandma. I no longer felt invisible.

Yolanda took her scant belongings to the basement of the Tivoli house and lived for a year and a half in the dank guestroom, cooking and cleaning and looking after Isabel while I taught and resumed my full-time life at the college. My mom was displaced, but she was content—satisfied that she had answered the call of her son and granddaughter, who orbited around her *nonna* like a tiny moon. Whenever

I brought Isabel back from an outing, she would burst into
the house calling *"Nonnie!"* and hurl herself into my mom's
arms, who would coo, *"dammi la manuzza, bella"*—"give me
your little hand, beautiful one"; or *"Tesoro mio, bentornata!"*—
"Welcome back, my treasure!" Then Isabel's eyes would
light up, her fatigue dispelled, the world once again warm
and familiar, as my mother spooned water into her mouth
from a cup or blew soothing air onto the piping hot soup that
she offered Isabel. Within minutes, Isabel would fall asleep,
so comforted by her grandmother's embrace that her body
would shut down and rest, nestled as she was into the safest
of all possible worlds.

Isabel was not the only one bonding with Nonnie. As I shared
a coffee with my mother in the morning or washed dishes together with her at night, I heard for the first time many of the
stories of her past. She would talk for hours about her childhood
and marriage in Calabria, the pleasures and challenges of raising a large family with little money and alongside a devoted but
imperious husband. I was astonished by how much she was the
child of tradition—literally a vessel for its accumulated wisdom.
I came to understand and finally value her fatalistic worldview,
which was religious without being spiritual. She took God's existence as a fact of life that neither warmed her heart nor inspired
her thoughts. He was there controlling the universe just as the
sun controlled the orbit of the planets, and His world was fundamentally one of struggle and suffering. *"Dio proveda, figlio mio,"*
she would say whenever we spoke of the challenges Isabel was

facing in this unusual family structure, "May God provide, my son." Her expectations of what the divinity should provide were, to put it mildly, on the low side. Once, when discussing a friend of hers who had, in my mom's opinion, foolishly abandoned her tyrannical husband, she said, *"Non la menava, 'n beveva o 'n andava cu altre fimmine, ma cosa voleva?"*—"He didn't hit her, didn't drink or sleep with other women—what more could she want?" In her life of frequent obstacles and scant choices, a woman's task was to endure her lot and protect what she had. Especially her children. She would have given limb and life for Isabel and me without thinking. Indeed, she gave us life at a time when all I knew was death, and when Isabel needed the nourishment that only a mother figure could have provided. I had spent much of my life running from my family's traditional ways, but what had been oppressive to me in my youth and earlier adulthood was now bounty for me and my daughter. I was finally able to embrace the gift that was the centuries of Calabrian maternal wisdom Yolanda Luzzi carried in her five-foot, two-inch, one-hundred-and-ten-pound frame.

From the time Isabel was born, I occupied myself with what I understood to be a father's duties: I saved for her college education; I researched her preschool programs to be sure they were reputable and safe. And I tried my best to ensure she was eating nutritious foods—though admittedly I failed much of the time as my mom indulged Isabel with saccharine delights that set my teeth on edge. I had looked forward my entire adult life to being a father, and these practical tasks made me feel like I was doing my job. But something was missing, some deeper connection to Isabel's well-being that could not be articulated with a college savings account and Kindermusik sing-alongs. I felt that I was coming up short by my inability to fill the role of Isabel's mother as well as her father. And yet, I didn't even know what that meant except in the context of my own mother, whose self-sacrifice was extreme. Surely I hadn't expected Katherine to mother as Yolanda did. But on some unconscious level I was in thrall to this notion of motherhood as complete surrender for the child: the ability to turn the focus of your day toward your child's needs instead of your own, and to do it all with love and no resentment. I couldn't get there. I had not yet reached that stage of parenting that Dante celebrates in the Virgin Mary of his *Divine Comedy*. It's not that Dante wanted us to look to the Virgin as a guide to mothering. What he meant, I believe, is that there is a love and joy in sacrifice—in learning to put someone else's needs before your own and relishing the role.

My mom had always struck me as one of the most self-realized people I knew. She had lived the fullest of lives precisely because she had lived a life of the most generative love—a love, like Mary's in Dante's heaven, that gave of itself endlessly and selflessly. The purity of Mary's love became a symbol to me of the love a parent feels for his child—an instinctual feeling that had been crushed by grief and that I was now trying to restore.

Dante called the Virgin Mary a torch of charity; different

fires burned within me. In the summer before moving into our new home in Tivoli, I took Isabel for a ride one night in the pretty coastal village of Stonington Borough in Connecticut. On the way home, I stopped for some takeout at a Mexican restaurant. I was dressed casually in sweatshirt and sneakers, while all around me coiffed young couples sipped margaritas and dipped tortilla chips in guacamole. I picked up my order and was walking to the car with Isabel when a young mother in her thirties breezed past me with her husband and two children. She was sandy-haired, athletic, and naturally attractive, and she was laughing at something that her youngest boy had said to her. Desire pulsed through me. There was someone out there like her, I swore to myself, someone not yet attached who could complete Isabel and me. Long after I had accepted Katherine's death, I still was unable to accept that I no longer had a wife and that my daughter did not have a mother. I fell easy prey to fleeting domestic images like the lithe, laughing woman and all the domestic bliss I imagined her to embody.

Worshiping these false images of mothers instead of actually learning how to mother my child, I let the family that we were supposed to be, Isabel and I together, die a little each day.

"I JUST CAN'T DO THIS . . ."

"Joe, you have no choice."

My friend was right.

I had been trying hard in my *vita nuova* to find love. I asked close friends as well as acquaintances to set me up; I went to parties where I was certain there would be single women; I went to parties where I doubted there would be a single woman but wanted to double-check just in case. There was nothing carefree, fun, or sexy about any of it. Dating became a tedious job. I began to doubt if I was looking for love. Part of me believed that Katherine was my once-in-a-lifetime *grande amore*. Even if I met someone else, I would remain eternally faithful to her in spirit if not in body. Was it possible to make room for another? I wondered. Can you have more than one soul mate in life? Plagued by these hypotheticals, I persevered halfheartedly to find a woman I could love.

With my friend looking over my shoulder and making sure I followed through, I pressed the "accept" button and became one of Match.com's millions of lonely hearts.

With time I began to rediscover the kind of love that Guido Cavalcanti wrote about: the love for a tender woman's touch. Soon after buying my new home in Tivoli, I began to see an actress who lived in a musty second-story walkup in New York's East Twenties. Siena was intensely articulate, intelligent, but very cynical—she once quoted me the line from the movie *Perfect Stranger*, "Show me a beautiful woman, and I'll show you a man who's tired of sleeping with her" (although, true to the original source, she used a more graphic term than "sleeping"). She slept beneath an imposing skull replica that looked down on my body with what I imagined not to be goodwill. The skull seemed to be Siena's protector, warning me that I had better satisfy the lady of the manor. I tried not to look into the empty eye sockets. Meanwhile, this lady of Madison Square Park was giving me something that I hadn't truly experienced since my time with Katherine: Siena made my body feel good again. I insisted on believing, in my usual clumsy way, that there was something more to our occasional but hair-raisingly satisfying physical relationship. But Siena's actions suggested otherwise: one night she was going to attend an awards ceremony, and there was no mention—not even a veiled hint—that I might be her date. Ours was not the kind of relationship that went out much in public.

Katherine's death had made intimacy terrifying for a long time, dating back to those exploding-heart embraces with Astrid. But Siena helped me to return to what Guido called love's trodden—and deeply physical—ways.

I understood that this interlude would end sooner than later, so I kept looking for someone to rebuild my family with, someone who could pick up Isabel and me where exile's bow had so violently shot us. My usually romantic nature was brutally rational on this: the person I settled with had to be family-minded. Without realizing it, I was following Dante's model in *Paradiso*: looking for a mother figure to nurture my child and absorb my suffering.

IN CHOOSING MY ID FOR Match.com, I avoided the open-ended (johndoe), the clever (youneverknow), the sentimental (giveloveatry), and the crass (guysjustwannahavefun). I went instead

for something cerebral and coded: posthoc7. Any woman attuned to the resonances of my Latin term, I thought in full
pedantry, was my kind of woman. The rest of my profile was
a study in understatement. I filled in only the most essential
data, such as height and weight and education, leaving everything else of substance blank, including income and religion.
I figured that the few items that I bothered to list said it all:
widower, father, PhD, just enough coordinates to let an enterprising potential partner fill in the blanks.

I soon met a woman who seemed hatched in algorithmic
heaven. Clarissa loved children and was a pediatrician, in her
late thirties, a Harvard graduate, and tired of being single.
Of course she was, and so was I—that was the problem with
Match: those of us of a certain age were approaching it from
a position of weakness, admitting that our lives were broken,
or incomplete, and in need of virtual enhancement. That's
how it felt to me, anyway, someone who had grown up—
like Clarissa, like most of the women I would meet through
Match—in an analog age. A time when you met your partner,
your spouse, or your love interest through friends, at the laun-
dromat, in the campus center, walking the dog, on a 5K run,
or at a wine tasting—anywhere but in the Match mall with
its cute profiles, clever opening remarks, and empty promises. I had never been on so many dates with people from so
many different walks of life—the sailor from Newport, the
teacher from Providence, and the lawyer from Newburgh are
just a small professional and geographical sampling—and yet

I never felt farther from finding what I was looking for. Match made me nostalgic for my failed love with Astrid. At least I had been on familiar ground with her. We were introduced by a mutual friend, and we were connected by our academic worlds and shared heartbreak. Now, looking for love had become online shopping.

The pages of Match's headshots—women in formal evening wear, drunken ladies hoisting margaritas, magazine models posted as an unconvincing alias—required immediate and categorical judgments. This one was too short; that one didn't know how to spell; this one wore too much makeup, that one too little; this one made too much money, that one too little. I too was on the receiving end of judgment: I didn't list my income, which made me of questionable financial independence; I had a daughter; I was in my forties; and I was a *widower*. In the future-oriented world of Match.com, I had a past. Worse still, I carried with me the sign of the grave. If ever there were a filter to separate the serious contenders from the ephemeral, here it was. No woman would bother with somebody carrying so much baggage, I told myself, unless she was truly interested (or just as needy as I was).

Clarissa and I agreed to meet at Al Forno, a restaurant on Providence's waterfront, during one of my visits to Rhode Island with my mom and Isabel. She asked me which part of the city I lived in. I told her that I had listed Providence as my address because I spent a lot of time there—which was rubbish. I had listed it because I was embarrassed to be on Match.com, and didn't want anyone in Tivoli or Westerly to discover me on the site. I was undercover.

Like me, Clarissa had enjoyed a comfortable life because of her professional success. She talked warmly about the child patients in her medical practice and openly admitted that she was ready to find someone to share her life. When we said good-bye in the parking lot of Al Forno we kissed briefly, and, as I inhaled her delicious scent through her clumps of curly brown hair, I promised that I would call her. We saw each other again for drinks in Narragansett at Turtle Soup a few weeks later, after Hurricane Irene had ravaged the Rhode Island coast. As we talked, the ocean quietly lapped the rocks along the shore, looking oddly docile under its coat of storm debris. Clarissa was lovely and intelligent, and everything she said was just right. But I knew in my heart that I couldn't become the person she was looking for. Not for her, not for the others I met on Match. None of them were from my village—neither my Westerly world that Katherine joined so effortlessly nor the campus culture that was my natural habitat. More to the point, I had met Katherine and even Astrid in physical time and space; we literally shared common ground, not a website. The algorithmic happenstance that put me in contact with Clarissa and others felt forced and false, unnatural. I could simply never accept it. Dante had once tried to get over Beatrice's death with the aid of numerology, patterning his meetings with her on the blessed number nine. Just as this number failed to mitigate his grief, so too did the ones and zeros of my computer's inexorable binary logic fail to spit out the love of my life.

That first summer I signed up for Match I visited the Watch Hill beaches in Westerly with Siena, she of the vigilant skull. It was the last glorious weekend of August, and I was walking with her and Isabel along a coastline to where the public, sandy beach ended and the private, rocky one began. We crossed the boundary with Isabel in tow. I had grown up seeing the rock barrier in summer and had never dared to cross it before. On the other side of it, a completely different stretch of coast opened up, a dazzling expanse of mansions and white umbrellas. *Is this what love is*, I asked myself as I held Siena's hand to stabilize us on the slick rocks, *exploring new worlds together, even ones you thought were familiar or forbidden?* There wasn't a cloud in the sky. I was as fit as I had ever been from all the tennis I'd been playing. There was a compelling and gorgeous woman in a bathing suit holding my hand as she walked beside me. My other hand held the soft and tiny hand of my little girl. We three looked, to the world, like a family. *If only this picture were the stuff of real life*, I thought. *If only this idyll could become a home.* Though trained to read closely and think deeply, I would swoon at these seductive, grief-addled snapshots that hid life rather than revealed it.

When I thought back to my time with Katherine, on that first day she arrived in North Carolina, I felt the same fullness of expectation and desire, but with Katherine it was the beginning of our life together. Five years later, on Westerly's beaches, it was not the beginning of anything. It was only a brief respite from my loneliness. By the time fall rolled around, the beach had become too cold to visit, and my story with Siena had already gone the way of the changing seasons. Our summer walk had been only that, a stroll on a holiday weekend, just before the sunbathers left the beaches.

A few months later I read a profile on Match of a woman with long brown hair and large inviting blue eyes. She too had once found love and was looking for it again. She was about my age, an educator, and she had a young child. She was also a widow. Careful to control the surge of hope pulsing through me, I reached out from behind my posthoc7 mask and began the typical email banter. Soon enough, we agreed to meet for a drink—at Al Forno, where I had succeeded in impressing Clarissa before evaporating from her life like morning fog. Emilia showed up in a hand-knit sweater and cargo pants, looking as fresh and warm as she had looked in her profile photo. She told me about the car accident that had taken her husband, the love of her life, just as she became pregnant with their daughter. I told her my own story, which was much more recent. Emilia had built a life for herself and her child, working as an English teacher at a prep school. She showed me a picture of her daughter, a smiling child of ten who loved to read. She had made it to the other side of grief and could tell that I was still in transit.

We ordered wood-fired pizza and drank southern Italian red wine. After dinner, I walked her to the car. She drove a Volvo—"the safest car I could find"—and, after embracing in solidarity, we made plans to see each other again. It was late December, the dead of a New England winter, and the dead center of my season of grief and mourning. Katherine had been gone three years now. My life had settled into a stalemate. Emilia drove away, and I sat down in my car and suddenly, unexpectedly, began to weep, spilling an Aegean Sea of sorrow like Ulysses as I released the tears that I had been unable to let go of when I received the news of Katherine's death. Here I was, in a Providence parking lot, hundreds of miles from home, pursuing a new life that refused to appear. Even Katherine's death felt remote by now. I was far away from my greatest love and felt even farther from any future love. I knew I would never call Emilia again, no matter how pretty and kind she was, no matter how much she could have offered me and my daughter. Listening to her story, I heard my own story. She became the mirror of my own sorrow. The world had brought me to my knees in Poughkeepsie's Saint Francis Hospital that cold November morning. I had begged the neurosurgeon, begged God, to keep Katherine alive. But she was gone forever, and now I was fumbling in the dark for directions back to Westerly from Providence, looking for the highway entrance in a maze of one-way streets as I sobbed in my car.

On the drive home that night, I passed a series of roads with allegorical names, Benevolent, Hope, Transit, all of them pointing to the mother's love that Isabel needed from me. Instead, I kept looking for a new wife, a new life, a *vita nuova* in a shopping mall of love—an outsider to the bond that was blazing between my child and her *nonna*, the woman whose Calabrian womb had first lit my world with love.

CHAPTER 8

Fathers and Sons

"Once upon a time . . . there was *un pezzo di legno*," "a piece of wood."

It was a month before Isabel's birth, and Katherine and I were sitting together on the couch of our apartment in Tivoli. We had lifted her shirt to admire the beach ball of her abdomen while I read from *Pinocchio* to her womb. I said the words slowly, holding the Italian double consonant on my tongue. I wanted our baby to pick up the rhyming vowels and sumptuous rhythms of Dante's Tuscan, modernized in the famous children's story by Carlo Collodi. I hoped that the child would recognize my voice as the vibrations from my mouth passed through the womb and into the amniotic fluid. Mine were the unknowing and anticipatory thoughts of an expecting father: Would the baby be a boy or girl? Will he like tennis when he grows up? Will she look like her mother? I was blithely unaware of the demands of childrearing. Katherine and I had settled into the quiet rhythm of our lives while we waited for the baby's arrival on an expected delivery date of January 6, 2008.

After Isabel defied the odds to make it into the world, I went from taking her life for granted to being unable to look at her without my heart racing. I had become her biological father in a grisly instant; becoming her actual father would take years. I hadn't reflected on what fatherhood meant before her birth. It seemed like one of those roles— son, friend, husband—that I would embrace and figure out when the time came. But when it arrived suddenly and violently, I was clueless. My preconceived notions of a father's roles—breadwinner, patriarch, protector—belonged to an outdated playbook. And I will never know what course my development as a father would have taken had Katherine survived.

This situation called for immense courage and imagination— qualities that were hard to come by in the Underworld.

IN THE YEARS WHEN I turned to Dante's poem for guidance, I also wanted to learn as much as possible about the man behind the words. The *Enciclopedia dantesca* (*Dante Encyclopedia*), a six-volume whale of a book published in Rome in the 1970s, covers every aspect of Dante's life and work, including his family tree. It lists his long-suffering spouse, Gemma Donati, who had to stand by as Dante dedicated all his poetry to Beatrice without ever once mentioning her—such were the conventions of medieval courtly love, which forbid the true lover from writing about his wife in poems celebrating unattainable love with extramarital muses. The family tree names Dante's four children, including Pietro and Jacopo, who in true Italian style turned their father's genius into a family business, as they both wrote influential commentaries on his work. The branches of the family tree arch downward from Dante to his father, Alighiero degli Alighieri, and encompass Cacciaguida, the ancestor who predicts Dante's exile in *Paradiso*. But the tree doesn't stop at this eleventh-century ancestor—it reaches all the way back to Adamo, the Biblical Adam, late of the Garden of Eden and a central character in *Paradiso*, where Dante calls him the *padre antico*, "ancient father." The editors actually place a question mark after his name, suggesting that Dante may in fact have been related to Adam. Since there is no place for humor in Dante scholarship—just as, oddly enough, there is no place for humor in a work with the word "comedy" in its title—the question mark seems to appear in all earnestness. And why wouldn't it? Dante was a man who took his father figures, and fatherhood, very seriously.

Dante never mentions his actual father, Alighiero, in his writing—but his other characters do. Forese, the scandalous sonneteer whom we meet in *Purgatorio* and one of Dante's friends, wrote that Dante's father was "*tra le fosse*"—"among the pits"—in the Florentine prison reserved for debtors. And indeed, Alighiero played a dangerous professional game: he was a moneylender, a practice that was reviled on Christian grounds, but which helped make Florence into Europe's first financial juggernaut. For his part, Dante loathed the moneylenders, punishing them in the seventh circle of Inferno as those who do violence against themselves, usurers who reject God's plan calling for labor and who seek to earn money from money itself. Despite the confusion over Forese's cryptic line, the image of Dante's father as a businessman intent on furthering his family's interests at all costs endures, suggesting his link to the furtive practices dear to the banking class in Dante's age. What we do know is that Alighiero had little in common with his famous son, and the poet seems to have found little in his father's life worth celebrating.

So Dante reinvented a new father figure with his poetry.

IN 2009, MY FRIEND JENNIFER DAY, who had been in the hospital with me as I received news of Katherine's death, died of heart failure on the third floor of Bard's Seymour Hall, just above my office on the second floor. I was coming from a film screening that warm spring evening when I noticed a flurry of ambulance and police cars outside my building. I knew immediately what had happened. Jen had been suffering from inexplicable but constant heart troubles the entire semester and had just returned to campus after an extended leave. Tragedy's red sirens were once again alight.

Jen had a two-year-old son called Tristram, in French the "sad one." He was born a few months before Isabel, and when Jen and Katherine were pregnant together, we imagined these babies would become bosom playmates. But Isabel and Tristram would hardly ever meet. Jen's husband, Rob, was a friend of mine, and after her death I tried to be there for him and offer him what comfort I could. But there was too much sorrow between us. It was suffocating for me, and I quietly distanced myself from him. As Rosalind had taught me, widows and widowers don't need to say anything to understand each other— but sometimes that understanding is too thick for intimacy to take hold, as I had learned on my date with the equally star-crossed Emilia from Match.com.

The day of Katherine's death, Jen offered to nurse Isabel with her milk. Tristram was six months old at the time. Jen was living her dream, nurturing her child from her own body, and she was willing to do the same for Isabel. But I couldn't bear the thought of another person, even if she was a loving friend, fulfilling the role that should have been Katherine's, so I opted for the sterile world of bottles and formula.

Shortly after bringing Isabel home from the hospital, Jen came over with Tristram to visit Isabel, my mom, and me in Tivoli. She was a promising scholar of Russian literature, an expert on the magical city of Saint Petersburg, and one of the college's most beloved teachers. But on the day of her visit, she was, above all, a mother. Ever since her child was born she had a serene aura about her. She had fully integrated her life as a scholar and her role as a mother, radiating the kind of contentment that comes to those who are doing their life's chosen work. And then, just months later, she left us.

To commemorate her death, my colleagues and I planted a dogwood tree outside the language building, sprinkling her ashes at the spot where she had inspired so many students. I would walk past the tree every day on my path from the parking lot to my office, and, as much as I tried, I could never find any solace by her grave. It was impossible to shake the feeling that Jen had been cheated. Students and faculty scurry past her grave, thinking of exams to study for, conference papers to prepare, financial aid forms to fill out, children to pick up from school. Rob recently remarried and left upstate New York to build a new life for himself, his wife, Tristram, and their new child in Berkeley, on the opposite coast of his late wife's final resting place. We rarely speak of Jen on campus, and her presence has become like the tree that commemorates her—something beautiful and overlooked at the periphery of our lives.

A year after Jen's death, the college held a symposium in her honor, and I read a passage from a Russian novel, Turgenev's *Fathers and Sons*, about when the character Nikolai Petrovich looks back on the life he shared with his late wife and then asks, "Where had it all vanished? . . . These sweet first moments, why could one not live an eternal, undying life in them?" I chose these words because they captured the quiet, graceful poetry that Jen had made of her brief life. Katherine's death had obliterated me; Jen's confused and angered me. I had chosen the passage as much for myself—and for Rob—as I had for Jen. Nikolai Petrovich wasn't just thinking about his late wife as he wandered through the woods. It was also the day that his son returned home from college, with ideas of progress and change that would distance him from his childhood and close relationship with his father. As he reflected on his late wife, Petrovich also wondered whether he was losing his son. The passage is about the distance that grows between fathers and sons, a feeling that I knew all too well. I had never really known my father as a person, but rather as a powerful Mussolini-of-the-manor whose approval I always sought but rarely gained.

While I was studying for my master's exams in the 1990s, I moved back in with my parents for a while. My father would often drive me to and from our home in Westerly to my job at a copy shop on the University of Rhode Island campus. The drive took forty-five minutes, and for the length of the trip he wouldn't say a word to me. He would just stare ahead, grimly focused on the drive, listening to Salty Brine spin the oldies on a crackling AM radio station as we rolled past the university's turf farms. In saying nothing, the ride said it all: growing up, we never had a single father-son conversation that, I imagined with wild jealousy, all my other friends enjoyed with their dads. Yet I revered him. My

father had an aura, with the absolute command he ema-
nated at home, and the astonishing care and perfectionism
he put into everything he did, from his manicured garden
and oversize vegetables to his legendary homemade wine.
Even the waves of his salt-and-pepper hair fell perfectly into
place, as if frightened of disobeying him. I realize now what
I could not fathom then: we were from different universes,
and understanding between us was impossible, as we spoke
no common language, figuratively and literally (he with his
broken English, I with my fragmented Calabrian, a dialect
of Italian). By my midtwenties I had graduated college and
held a series of half-baked jobs, just like the one at the copy
shop; by his midtwenties he had endured extreme poverty,
fought for Italy in World War II, and survived years as a military internee in Nazi Germany. The ease of my life, a sign
to him that I was not a serious person, embarrassed him.

Once, when I played for the number two spot on my high
school tennis team, he showed up at the Weekapaug courts
in his Chevy Malibu—the same one in which we would ride
in silence. He had sworn to me before the match that he was
going to pull me off the courts, *"davant' a tutti"*—"in front of
everyone"—because I was burning holes in my sneakers that
he could not afford to replace. He wanted me to play in the
same heavy steel-toe Sears work shoes that he used for his land-
scaping. I tried to stare down my archrival, a cocky doctor's
son who had a tennis court in his backyard—but I couldn't
focus on his white Rossignol racket, as my head swam with the

image of my father haunting the parking lot. He never left his car that day, silently raging in the driver's seat while I played. In between serves I peered out of the corner of my eye to see him and my mother both sitting expressionless in the distance, two Calabrian ghosts surreally transplanted to a lovely seaside enclave of driftwood houses and thick coastal woods. She must have talked him out of his plan: after the match he drove away from the courts without so much as a word to me.

Needless to say, I lost in straight sets.

I swore to myself that I would be a different father, one who engaged with his children, guided and supported them through life, showed them his love. Then I found myself in a dark wood of unusual configuration, co-parenting with my mom and separated forever from my wife. It became clear to me that my imagined role as a father had been based on the corollary of Katherine as a mother, rather than that of Isabel as my daughter.

By 2011, four years into widowerhood, I passed a grim milestone: I had lived without Katherine for as long as I had lived with her, as the period of her death matched that of our time together. I had spent over one thousand days with her, over one thousand days without her. And over one thousand days trying to be a father to a motherless daughter. With each day, just like in the famous story, that daunting number of absences would continue to grow—one thousand and one days and counting, an outsize, make-believe number that suggested grief's awesome scale.

The brutal math of grief was now weighted more toward death than life. But looking at the balance of life with Isabel, the weight would begin to shift again toward life. I just wasn't there yet. I was still entrenched in a world without fatherhood.

I CANNOT BLAME MY SHORTCOMINGS as a father on Pasquale Luzzi, who was too remote to be a role model. And worshiping him—which in this case also meant fearing him—was a far cry from being able to emulate him. In *Inferno* 11, Dante describes how the upper, less terrifying part of hell receives those who suffered from failure of the will—sinners who wanted to act a certain way but could not. I had the best of intentions with Isabel, but I could not abandon my own needs to carve out a life for the two of us. I kept seeking, hunting, clawing for that magical third who would rescue us: Astrid's instant family, one of Match.com's infinite options, a successful blind date set up by a friend. Although none of these came to fruition, I kept holding on to my fairy-tale image of fatherhood as something that would come to life when I had a new mother beside me. A failure of will prevented me from going it alone.

Early in my relationship with Astrid, we planned to spend the weekend at her Brooklyn loft. Isabel, who was now a year old, would be coming along—one of the rare times that she accompanied me on a visit to Astrid. The entire week before our little trip, my mom and sisters fretted: Where would Isabel be sleeping? Would I remember to feed her at the appointed times? What if Isabel fell ill? All their worrying had reduced me, an edgy enough father, into a quaking mess. It was a big test in my relationship with Astrid and of my competence in caring for Isabel on my own. Time and again I had shown up to see her without my daughter in tow, and her patience was wearing thin. Our future seemed to hang on this weekend. My mother and sisters watched helplessly as I whisked Isabel to Brooklyn for our fateful trip.

When it came to bedtime our first night there, Isabel would have none of it. She cried and cried, wracking sobs. She was inconsolable. I did everything humanly possible to soothe her, rocking her in my arms, whispering into her ear, promising rides on swings and seesaws. Nothing worked. She only ratcheted up the shouts and tears. Astrid looked on helplessly, our would-be romantic evening reduced to an exhausting and sleepless night for all of us. I had heard that level of pitch and discomfort in my daughter's voice only as an infant when she had screamed into my chest at three in the morning, just weeks after Katherine had died.

Of course, Isabel was crying that night in Brooklyn because she was used to routine, and this was the rare instance when I had pulled her from all she knew in her Westerly-Calabria bubble. She was in a different space, and it made her afraid and uncomfortable. Had I been more attuned to her needs, I would have understood what her discomfort was all about. I was forcing her to be present in my life for this special weekend with Astrid. I had it backward: I should have always been present in her life and merely extended that into our visit to Brooklyn, and the blip of my would-be romantic getaway with Astrid should have been just another family trip by a seasoned dad and his well-traveled daughter.

By three in the morning, instead of subsiding, Isabel's wails only increased. When I decode those screamed messages to me now, I hear them say, *Please*, basta *with the nonsense about the playground—just assume your role and be my father.*

DANTE HAD SPENT HIS LIFE looking for a father figure. First, there was his older-brother figure Guido Cavalcanti, but Dante could never spend his life in the electric air of grief that was Guido's chosen home. Then there was Brunetto Latini, but his ego was too outsize for the generosity of spirit that fatherhood demands. Finally there was Virgil, a great father indeed, but one whose lack of Christian faith made it impossible for him to guide Dante through heaven. Only in *Paradiso* could fatherhood ripen to its full role.

O my leaf . . . I was your root.

With these words—and with this poetic re-creation of his family tree—Dante meets his ancestor, Cacciaguida degli Elisei, a twelfth-century crusader (born about 1091) who was Dante's great-grandfather four times over. The word "leaf" held a special resonance for Dante because it represented the cyclical nature of human time: the waxing and waning of generations, a melancholic contrast to the everlasting divine. Dante chose Cacciaguida partly out of his own insecurity: as one who came from *"poca nobiltà di sangue"*—"minor noble blood"—Dante wanted to overcome the stigma of his money-lender father and show readers that he came from an illustrious family line. A ferocious warrior for the Christian cause, proud Cacciaguida had impeccable hereditary credentials.

Cacciaguida, Dante writes, lived in a Florence that was sober and chaste, filled with virtuous women who scorned makeup and jewelry. The scholar Teodolinda Barolini called the fashions of Dante's idealized Florence "caveman chic," and Cacciaguida's description does come across as farfetched: in his Florence one nobleman goes around wearing a belt of leather and bone, while others are content to don unlined animal skins. It's not surprising that Dante would create so extravagant—and skewed—a picture of this primitive Florence that never was. He had fallen prey to the great enabler of grief and handmaiden of mourning—a disease that itself was an invention, that of nostalgia.

In 1688, a nineteen-year-old Swiss medical student, Johannes Hofer, began to notice the strangest things. A group of Swiss mercenaries stationed in France—a band of rugged, coarse, and unsentimental men, paid killers—were suffering from fainting, high fever, indigestion, stomach pain, even death, and for no explicable reason. Hofer came up with a phrase for it: "the sad mood born from the desire to return to one's homeland." The Swiss soldiers he treated were hardy mountaineers now marooned in the French lowlands. The thought of their beloved mountains seemed to make them literally sick to their stomach. The military doctors surmised that the soldiers were brain-damaged or that they had been overexposed to the constant banging of cow kettles in the Alps, damaging their eardrums and brain cells. Some even prescribed leeches; a Russian army officer went farthest of all, burying a homesick soldier alive in the hopes of curing him. Hofer knew better. He understood that the illness afflicting the soldiers was truly psychosomatic: a sickness of the mind that had migrated to the body. And so Hofer coined a term—an old-sounding term that was in fact young: *nostalgia*, from the Greek *nostos* and *algos*: the pain of homecoming. The Swiss mercenaries were dying of homesickness.

Centuries before the term nostalgia was created, Cacciaguida describes a Florence that was hatched from Dante's longing to return to his forever lost homeland. Like all imaginary homelands, especially the ones that we desperately yearn for, the Florence that Cacciaguida praises never existed.

Dante would be able to return to Florence only through his poetry, which would re-create the sounds and smells of his childhood home and the Tuscan language that brings *The Divine Comedy* to life. Immersing himself in his epic poem, he discovered the means to vanquish nostalgia.

Cacciaguida had taught him about his ancestry, where he came from—but only poetry, his rediscovery of the power of art, could teach him where he was going.

MY FATHER HAD BEEN DEAD for over a decade before Isabel was born. He was as remote to me, in many ways, as Cacciaguida was to Dante: he was a legendary figure who taught me about origins by giving me all the material I needed to write the story of our family, which became the book *My Two Italies*. In the greatest compliment I received about that book, a reader told me that it was written without nostalgia. In no sense does it express the desire to return to a lost childhood and a lost homeland that no longer existed. Nostalgia feasts on grief and mourning, which erect monuments to former or imagined lives, dreams once shared. And now nostalgia was clouding my vision. But it was nostalgia for a fatherhood I never experienced—not from my own father, nor from my own life with Isabel.

My mother once said something about my father that shook the foundation of my memory. She told me that in Italy he had been a different person, capable of great joy and spontaneity—everything but the tortured, autocratic, and difficult person I had known from my childhood in the 1970s and 1980s up to his death in the 1990s. He had left everything he knew and loved in Italy to build a life for his family in America: his family and friends in Calabria, its breathtaking landscape that he toiled as a farmer. In the U.S. he would only know the insides of factories and sixty-hour workweeks. He had embraced his exile, discounting all present happiness for the future of his family. Dante too had embraced exile, making it the bird's-eye view on human life that enabled him to let go of all his earthly attachments and attain true wisdom. I used to think of my family's journey from southern Italy to America as a narrative of immigration, one that saw them trade up their poor village struggles in the Old Country for a solid middle-class life in the new world. But listening to my mom tell me about my father's pain after leaving his homeland, I understood that I had only half of the story right. He had suffered, just like Dante, the trauma of exile.

In *Paradiso* 17, when Cacciaguida predicts Dante's exile and tells him that he will henceforth eat salty bread, he gives us a visceral detail of what life away from home will be like: a disgusting meal that no Florentine would ever willingly ingest. Life in the United States was one endless loaf of salty bread for my father, but he ate it, for us, his children, so that we would have opportunities he never had. My father had been a sub-sistence farmer in Calabria, plowing the stingy earth for little yield and harvesting sparse crops of chestnuts. His entire life had been one of abject poverty, and by the early 1950s he found himself living with a wife and four young children in a stone hut with no bathroom on a Calabrian hillside. He could out-work everybody, and knew that across the Atlantic, relatives of his were making real money in the American Northeast. I don't know what he was thinking when he decided—for any and all major decisions in the household were his—to uproot his family and move them to a strange land that he would never accept, but I believe it had to do with his desire to break the cycle of poverty for his family. I never realized this growing up, but my father was a deeply ambitious man—it was what had driven him into the arms of his wife, Yolanda, a woman from a higher social class, and it was what had enabled him to sur-vive Nazi Germany. He was constantly imagining a different, better life for himself and those he loved. His American years were tormented, I believe, because the new world thwarted his dreams—yes, he made some money because of his exhausting factory work, and he was able to accrue personal savings and purchase real estate. But he never made it out of the factory, literally or figuratively. His dreams of owning his own business never made it to fruition, it was just too risky with six kids to feed and his poor English. Life in the U.S. was a grind—one that made the nostalgic pull of his lost Calabria, which in truth had been a land of even greater struggle, all the more seductive. He died longing for a Calabria that never was, because America never became the place he hoped it would be.

It amazes me now to think of what an idealist my father was, torn as he was between his quest for the American dream and his longing for the familiar sounds, smells, and tastes of his Calabria, which he re-created in every corner of Westerly, from the homemade wine he pressed in our cellar to the sprawling acres of fruits and vegetables he grew in our suburban home. I was his first American child, and could have presented him with an opportunity to learn about his new adopted country as it translated into the subjects I studied, the sports I played, and the culture that shaped me. But he would have none of it. He was too ferociously proud to bend an inch toward *l'America*, and as I unconsciously imbibed my surroundings, he quite consciously became more and more Calabrian. Part of his charisma was his dashing anachronism—he insisted on playing the old-world peasant even as his fellow Calabrian immigrants, men just as inveterately traditional as he, had begun to assimilate and bend to the American ethos. Instead of opening up his worldview at a time of profound change in American society in the sixties, seventies, and eighties, he sealed it hermetically shut, demanding that his children live according to the customs that existed only in his postwar Calabria. The women in our family were actively discouraged from careers and independence and forced into early marriages. When my unmarried sister Rose, at age twenty-seven, moved out because he would not let her take a trip with a female friend to Bermuda, he refused to speak with her for months. My father was the kind of man who, as his children were being delivered by my ever-pregnant mother, stayed clear of the hospital and chose instead to camp out at the Hilltop Social Club, drinking wine and dealing cards to his friends and four brothers throughout the birth of his two American children.

As a male child, I was subject to no such prohibitions as my sisters were, but, in a way, that made things harder. He simply did not know what to make of me. I visited him once at his social club, walking inside the infamous Hilltop to find him gambling with his fellow *calabresi* in the alcohol-soaked dimness, sealed in a sepulchral darkness on a sunny day. I was wearing paisley shorts that a college girlfriend of mine had jokingly let me borrow, and he shot me a look that nearly made my heart stop.

We are related by blood, that glance said to me, *and I can't change that. But I have no idea how I could have produced something like you, and I will not acknowledge this genetic link in public and among real men.*

We didn't discuss the incident afterward because we never discussed anything. It was just another episode in our intense and lonely connection. And yet, connected we were. During that same period when he would drive me in silence to and from the copy shop, I would occasionally have to return to New York to meet with my professors for work related to my master's degree. On these trips I would pack a separate duffel bag of books to go along with my luggage, and my father would always be the last to see me off with my load. By then he was in his early seventies in what would be the last few years of his life. The ferociously strong, squarely built man I had known growing up was now silvered, withered, and bent, prematurely aged by a massive stroke and forced to walk with a cane. He would hobble toward me with the bottom of his lip quivering as if he was trying to say something to me but just couldn't release the words. And then this deeply unsentimental, unemotional man—someone from whom trying to draw feeling had been like trying to squeeze water from a stone—would begin to weep in front of me as we said good-bye. His few words, "*statti accortu, figlio*"—"be careful, son"—seemed to come from the pit of his stomach, more a groan than a declaration, as I held his ravaged, slight body against my own. I was a young man who had never known any real challenge in life, so I couldn't interpret his silence, all the pain and sorrow of things not expressed but now emanating from his sobbing body. He was a man of few words, so perhaps he himself didn't even know what he wanted to tell me as I released him, choking back my own tears and heading out to make my train.

And so I grew up with a magnificent father figure—but no real dad.

WHEN ISABEL AND I FINALLY lived together in our little house in Tivoli (at first with my mom's help, later on our own), I discovered that the aspects of child care that had filled me with dread—preparing meals, arranging doctor's visits, packing diaper bags—quickly became welcome routine. True to my Westerly roots, I loved to take her shopping in the big box stores across the Hudson River from Bard. Pushing her through the aisles of Target or Wal-Mart in an elephantine red cart, I would fill up on whatever socks, underwear, toothpaste, and rain boots she needed. We had shopped together countless times—the Wal-Mart in Westerly, Rhode Island, was no different from the one in Kingston, New York. But now Isabel and I were back on home turf. We didn't need the sharks and dolphins of the Mystic Aquarium to entertain us, and I would no longer need to drop her off at Nonnie's as I used to do after the aquarium. Finally, as I balanced my shopping bags in one hand and hoisted Isabel into her car seat with the other, I felt like more than just her father—I was slowly becoming her dad.

When Dante saw his ancestor Cacciaguida for the first time in *Paradiso*, he felt flooded with a love that he had never before known—a love that combined Virgil's guidance with Beatrice's generosity. The loving guidance of a true father. And then Cacciaguida spoke:

O sanguis meus . . .

Yes, Dante must have thought, *the words should come in Latin— they should have the depth and resonance of that beautiful ancient language, the father of my Tuscan.*

I imagine him translating Cacciaguida's Latin into his native Tuscan: *O sangue mio.*

Oh my blood.

The blood that had joined my father and me in an instinctual bond—the kind that made for painful farewells and silent car rides—had slowly but inexorably suffused my connection with Isabel. I had learned that it's not enough to be born with this connection. It was my father's lifetime of devotion to his family that had united us, not the biological link that made me his natural son. And now, with Isabel, the link that fate had severed was being restored, with each trip together to Wal-Mart, each time I stopped running off to play tennis or go on dates with women I had no future with. I was finding a different kind of intimacy by bonding with her, once I realized that it wasn't so scary taking care of her on my own. I had been looking for a partner—someone to share my life with. And yet all along the person whom I should have prioritized was right in front of me, this beautiful light-haired three-year-old with the big gaps in her teeth. In tailoring my life to my child's, I was finally embracing all the chaos and energy that comes from true love— the kind that changes your life, sometimes violently.

The first years of Isabel's life, she would go to sleep at night with my mom, a ritual that continued when my mother came to live with us in Tivoli. Her grandmother would lie beside her on her miniature bed, holding her hand and soothing her so that she could surrender to sleep. Of course, Isabel became used to this, and so part of her daily routine became this nightly physical comfort from Grandma. In one of my first acts of true fatherhood after my mother had left us and returned to Rhode Island, I told Isabel that she was going to have to sleep by herself. You can imagine the fireworks. Isabel was just as disconsolate as she was that evening long ago in Brooklyn with Astrid and Anja, when I had similarly displaced her from the Nonnie-based routine that had defined her life. But this time was different. I would not swan off for a few days at Bard or in New York City; I would be with her in the morning, as I would be every night. As she bellowed, I told her that I loved her and that I would be close by while she slept. But she cried and cried. It was only exhaustion (hers) that settled the matter. By this time I was crying too because it anguished me to see my daughter suffer. I held my ground only because I knew that I was acting in her best interests, and, for the first time in my life, I was truly taking care of her.

I had imagined that fatherhood meant above all sacrifice, the giving up of the things you love for the one you love, a kind of ascetic affirmation of love in self-denial. How wrong I was. There was nothing of the sense of loss implied by sacrifice. The love I now felt for my daughter was the most satisfying, self-fulfilling I had ever known. In making her needs my own, I was finally able to let go of the searing loneliness and black hole of inwardness that had seized me since Katherine's death. Loving and taking care of Isabel had rescued me from myself—it wasn't sacrifice; it was sanctuary.

Three years earlier, I had held her sobbing body against my own in the middle of the night when exile's bow had shot us out of Tivoli and into my hometown of Westerly just weeks after we lost Katherine. Three years later, I dried her tears once again in Tivoli as Isabel struggled against having to sleep alone. But by now the arrow of exile had been returned to its source. As I held *il sangue mio* in the first home we had known, we were reunited after what felt to me like a light-year of separation. The savage math of grief can only be expressed in make-believe numbers like one thousand and one.

CHAPTER 9

Open Hours

O n a blustery spring day in 2013, the wind picked up as the violinist took the stage. In the large windows behind her, tall pines swayed on the hills of the Berkshires, their dull green and yellow forming a single band of color with her blond hair. The other musicians of the trio stood aside while she prepared to play the celebrated chaconne of Bach's Partita in D Minor.

"Alex Ross of the *New Yorker* has described the descending four-bar bass line as an exhale of grief," she announced to the audience. "Bach offers variations on this single theme no less than sixty-four times."

She paused to play the chords.

"He wrote the piece as a soliloquy for his recently deceased wife, Maria."

Bach left his home in 1720 to accompany the Duke of Köthen, his employer, to the Carlsbad spa and its healing waters. When he came home two months later, he discovered that Maria had suddenly died and was already buried in a Saxon churchyard. She had been in good health at his departure; the cause of her death remains unknown.

Isabel and I were sitting among an audience of about one hundred, in the living-room-turned-concert-hall of a large country home. Now five years old, Isabel fidgeted nonstop throughout the performance, whispering every five minutes that she was hungry and thirsty, as she tried gamely to endure our high-cultural Sunday.

"It's almost over, sweetie," I whispered back.

"When?"

"Five minutes."

"You said that five minutes ago."

I was running out of excuses—and juice boxes. Still, I managed to concentrate on the music enough to hear that the chaconne wasn't just a wail of grief. That sorrowful bass line was balanced by the piece's undulating rhythm. The word itself, *chaconne*, comes from the French word for a popular dance. Was it possible, I thought, that Bach's feelings about his late wife were *both* a wail of grief and a celebration of her life? Had Bach achieved Dante's challenge, to love somebody without a body, while accepting that, like the beloved herself, the earthly love that was once shared is gone forever? One of Bach's great interpreters, Arnold Steinhardt, called the chaconne "lusty." After my father died in 1995, my mother had stood by his coffin at the funeral home, her six children beside her, and cried, *"Guarda, Pasquà, guarda i figli che abbiamo fatto insieme!"*—"Look, Pasquale, look at the children we made together!" Was this the point of Bach's piece, I wondered, that the complexity of grief boils down to a combination of unspeakable sorrow and profound intimacy—and that you can continue to love someone even after the love you made together no longer electrifies the air?

By the end of the chaconne, Isabel was not just fidgeting—she was wrestling me. She twisted my head toward her, ready to lodge another complaint. I shifted in my seat and tried to take her in my arms to calm her. When I moved to pick her up by the stomach, I felt my pulse spike. Holding her taut and growing body gave me a visceral jolt: my daughter would never know the woman that she had once been part of. My heart was racing not because of Isabel's loss of her natural mother, but because I could feel the full force of my daughter's physical presence, the magical bundle of chaos and energy that she had become. She had made it to the other side, just barely. And now she was a robust little girl, with a Calabrian *testa dura*, a terrifying sweet tooth, raspy voice, and a fashion sense broad enough to encompass Laura Ashley dresses and camouflage cutoffs. Isabel at age five was a perfect blend of her biological origins, with her mother's fair skin, light hair, and fine bones to go along with her father's thick hair and strong features. The nurses had been right about her blue eyes turning brown, but otherwise Katherine's physical imprint was everywhere.

The sweet music coming off the strings made me think of Rosalind, of all the words of gratitude I wished I could express to her for treating me with such kindness when I ached for my former life and floundered in the job I had looked forward to my whole life, fatherhood. The sounds also brought to mind the chaplain Georgia and our brief, life-affirming conversation over coffee in the village of Red Hook near Bard, when all I could see were the red and brown leaves of the Underworld's eternal autumn.

Most of all, the violinist's whirring fingers, as they spun exquisite sounds from the strings, reminded me of the first words that she ever wrote to me two years earlier.

DEAR MR. LUZZI, *I would like to ask for a chance to meet when you have a moment. Do you keep open hours?*

The tone and diction threw me. My students didn't use old-fashioned terms like "open hours," nor did they tend to produce such polished and polite email requests. After a decade at Bard, I was more accustomed to receiving messages beginning with "Hey" and "Joe"—or "Hey Joe." I occasionally got the decorous "Professor Luzzi," but very rarely the wholesome "Mr." And very few of my correspondents used that delicious circuit breaker of politesse, the verb "would like," when asking for a

favor. The Romance linguist in me savored the construction—
"Never say 'I want' (*voglio*) in Italy," I repeated ad nauseam to
my students, "say 'I would like' (*vorrei*)." Say it, I would think,
the way Dante did around 1295, when he wrote to his best
friend, "*Guido, i' vorrei*"—"Guido, I would like," for you and me
to be cast under a spell and set sail together on a sea of love.
The woman's note was sparse and simple yet somehow sugges-
tive, in a charming, discreet way devoid of the usual Facebook
effusions and exclamation points. As Guido might have said,
Chi è questa che vèn?—Who is this lady arriving?

Just as fall classes were ending in December 2010, she
showed up in my office, a British beauty, dwarfed by an enormous double-instrument case containing her violin and viola.
I wasn't anticipating someone so lovely. She had large blue
eyes and an aquiline nose reigning over her delicate features.
In the volley of her clipped consonants and vowels, I gathered
that she had a position in the music program and was looking to take some undergraduate classes. A mutual friend had
given her my name, she told me, and suggested that she reach
out to me.

"I would like to take your Dante course," she announced.

I panicked. Something about her directness, the intensity of
her gaze, the clarity of her expression. My eyes weren't prepared for this much light. I told her that my class was full (when
it actually wasn't), and then I put on my best professorial game
face and shifted into the avuncular mode, recommending a
course taught by my least-threatening male friend. So-and-so

is a wonderful prof, I assured her, pointing to the course cata-
logue, and his such-and-such is one of our most popular classes.

"Well," she said, fixing me in her stare, "it's not so much the
class as the person teaching it, isn't it?"

The nails on her long delicate fingers were cut to stubs,
with callused tips suggesting years of toil on her violin. I
should have looked behind her open-ended words, but I was
still lost in a fog of incomprehension. Unmoored, I was still
looking for love in all the wrong, virtual places—hunting the
hare with the ox, as a favorite poet of mine once wrote. My
latest rabbit was a forty-something professor of English literature I had fallen hard for over lunch one summer afternoon
in Providence, after listening to her recite Emily Dickinson's
"I died for Beauty." We were set up by friends, and the match
looked promising on paper: we were both literature professors, had ties to upstate New York, thrilled to Wordsworth,
and captained our high school tennis teams. She had refined
bones, curly blond hair, and the baroque curves that can
only be described as zaftig. There was only one problem: she
lived and taught at a school in the Midwest, and, despite our
common zest for Romantic poetry and Bjorn Borg, we would
have made a horrible mixed doubles team. She had the good
sense to realize this; it took me a few months longer.

Meanwhile, the gentle, stub-nailed English apparition floated
into my office and then out of my life for what I thought was
forever. After our conversation ended, I wished her the best and
ushered her out, acting for all the world like a confident school-

master preaching the eternal truths, when I was actually a lost soul drawing imaginary angels in a street still paved with the memories of lost love.

FATE KEPT ITS CARDS CLOSE to the chest for a few months. Then, one cold, snowy day in Red Hook, less than a hundred yards from the diner where I had Cobb salad the morning after I brought Isabel home from Vassar Brothers, it flashed an ace. The English violinist walked in. This time, however, she didn't greet me so sonorously.

"*Joe!*" I heard her call out from across a crowded café as I ate my bagel and typed away on my computer. I had been coming to this café each morning after dropping Isabel off at her nearby nursery school. There she was, violin girl, as spritelike as ever, only this time her *Brideshead Revisited* demeanor dropped as she ambled over. Her car, a pale blue 1986 Volvo, was in the shop nearby, and she was on her way back to campus. We chatted about this and that, and agreed to stay in touch. But we had done that before— when I cloddishly recommended that she take my friend's Plato course, too opaque to register her invisible wink. I returned to my bagel and wondered what had happened, in just a few months' time, to make her respectful "Professor Luzzi" relax into a chummy "Joe." It could only mean one thing: if she had been interested in me before, now she was off me.

After forcing myself to wait forty-eight hours, I emailed

her on Friday at five p.m., inviting her to coffee at the café where we had just met. When I checked my office voicemail on Monday, I saw that, at the exact same time that I was emailing her, she had phoned me with a similar intent. Our wishes had intersected in time and space.

For the first time in four years, the stars aligned.

CLERMONT HISTORIC SITE, A ROLLING park along the Hudson, was once the home of the Livingston family, which included a framer of the U.S. Declaration of Independence, a U.S. minister to France, and a developer of steamboat technology. The park has maintained its colonial feel: the great house is fairly modest, at least by today's standards—it would barely qualify as a suburban McMansion—and the rough-hewn gardens and grounds recall a time when men and women lived at the mercy of nature. Sitting along its massive slopes, you can still imagine the mud-brown Hudson connecting humans to the sprawling metropolis ninety miles downriver.

A month after our messages crossed in cyberspace, the violinist and I met in Clermont on a raw April day. We had just passed a major milestone—my first full-on English breakfast, replete with runny eggs, fried tomatoes, and greasy sausage. My stomach was feeling the weight of this imperial diet, and I had stoically smiled as she dolloped the baked beans onto the pools of oil on my plate. Isabel and my mom were in Rhode Island and would return the week following. My date and I had the whole weekend to ourselves—for the first and basically the last time.

I was amazed that we had come this far. No more than fifteen minutes into our first date at the café, she repackaged the mantra that had haunted me after Katherine's death into a question:

"Do you find it meaningful?"

She was asking me about my work, as a teacher and a scholar, and I told her that yes, I did, but that lately I had learned that it wasn't enough, that I wanted to return to my earliest and first dream of being a writer—of books about life, not other books.

A week later, we met at Poet's Walk, a wooded enclave near the Bard campus. I told her of my failure to separate Isabel from my Calabrian family. I asked her if she knew "my story," something I could never ask of anyone from Match.com, because they only knew my profile, the cryptic phrases and meager data filed under my posthoc7 avatar. She nodded that yes, she knew, and then she told me how a mutual friend of ours had described to her the accident, my immediate return to the classroom, my years of a split life with its miserable commute between Bard and Westerly. And whereas the online world could consider the daughter of a single parent "baggage," our friend called Isabel "catnip"—a beautiful gift for anyone interested in the brooding Dante scholar, Professor Luzzi.

Then she told me her story: a musical family in London, boarding school in America at age fifteen, farewell to her homeland and childhood, her passion for Bach, the hustled opportunities of a musician's life. She told me about her cellist father in Bremen and her bohemian brother in London, the childhood outings to goose-crowded Verulanium Park by St. Alban's Cathedral, Easter egg hunts on Stanley Kubrick's sprawling estate in Hertfordshire, the bustling corridors of the Curtis Institute of Music in Philadelphia, a beloved mentor and her twin sister upstate. She was putting together a show at Bard, a collaborative dance and musical celebration of Bach's *Goldberg Variations*—would I please come?

I wanted to go, but wondered if it was wise to be seen with her in public. It was very difficult to guess her age. And I wasn't sure what her title, Artist-in-Residence, meant exactly—whether she was more a graduate student or a colleague. I knew that she was older than my students; but I didn't know if she had lived enough to understand my life and its special burdens. So I beat around the bush, asking her vague but age-specific questions, like what she thought of Jimmy Carter, only to receive an incredulous look and a reply that didn't really answer the question. One day while we were idling at a red light, I asked her about the fall of the Berlin Wall and what she remembered about it, since I knew that she had lived in Germany. The question was natural enough not to elicit a suspicious glance, and from her answer I finally learned that she was in her thirties. I exhaled and accelerated when the light turned green.

The weather that April day at Clermont was out of *Wuthering Heights*. The gray sky looked ready to erupt into torrential rain, and the spring wind bit through our coats. We laid out a blanket on an expanse designed for Heathcliff, one in which he would be reunited with his love and never let her go. The wind picked up, ripping the first leaves of the season prematurely from their buds and sprinkling us with their crisp yellow and green remains. A few drops fell from time to time, and it was cold enough that we had to huddle against each other for warmth. We didn't speak—it would have been difficult to hear with the wind anyway—while the park itself murmured the sounds of early spring. As we sat under the leaden sky and looked into the Hudson, I could feel our stories coming together—with one story missing. She still hadn't met Isabel.

It was all happening at once. I had started to make the first strides toward being Isabel's father, stocking the house with all she needed, and synchronizing my day according to her needs. Despite all these advances I made, my mom continued to live with us in Tivoli, and we still had a way to go until that time when Isabel would go to sleep without her Nonnie. But when I met the violinist I was not there yet. I knew that I needed to make a clean break, but I still doubted my abilities to go it alone. I still did not completely believe in myself as a dad and was still living in the shadow of Katherine's death—I didn't realize it at the time, but the two were related. In order truly to rebuild my life again, I would have to let go of death, but no act of will could get me there. Just as Dante could not get out of the dark wood without Beatrice's help, I too needed a loving hand to help me sever once and for all the bowstring that had first loosed exile's arrow.

A WEEK LATER, ON EASTER Sunday, I went to Rhode Island to pick up my mother and Isabel, where they had spent the week while I was away at a conference. The plan was that my mom would come back to Bard and stay with us for a month, then, once the Bard semester ended, she would return to Westerly for good, leaving Isabel entirely in my care. After four years, I would finally accept responsibility for Isabel on my own.

Easter in Rhode Island was subdued, almost funereal. My mother and sisters realized that they would be seeing less of Isabel as my relationship grew deeper with *"la donna inglese"*—"the English woman"—as my mom called her neutrally, waiting to see if she would pass muster. The violinist and I had been spending more and more time together. It had been a month since Poet's Walk, and I already knew that she was the woman I had been dreaming of finding. My family also knew that this was the best possible development for me and for Isabel. Yet they would miss their little girl. Through a wonder of love, care, and commitment, they had taken this four-pound, seven-ounce chickpea and protected her from an unspeakable grief, transforming a child of sorrow into a thriving, healthy child. When we had first moved back to Tivoli and I brought Isabel to the Bard Nursery School, she screamed so loudly that Nonnie had to stay with her the entire day while I went to teach. Normally the director of the school would have insisted that the caretaker leave the crying child to adjust, but in this case she saw that Isabel was truly inconsolable. And she knew our story. So Nonnie was asked to stay with Isabel there every day, all day, which she did for months on end. As time wore on, the director's patience thinned: Isabel still resisted potty training, and Nonnie had become a fixture at the school, stacking building blocks in the same playpen as a gaggle of well-adjusted three-year-olds. By Easter, I had to pull Isabel from Bard and enroll her in a new childcare center in Red Hook, without me or Nonnie beside her. I would drop her off in the morning and work in a café near the school—the same one where I met the violinist—then pick her up after lunch. We had finally established a routine and a rhythm, and the painfully shy and anxious infant that Isabel had been was evolving into a vibrant and adventurous toddler.

The whole Luzzi family had raised Isabel, and they anguished over their impending separation from her. Especially my mom. But she dared not breathe a word of her pain. Many times over the years she had told me that she prayed for the day when she would no longer be needed. That day had now come, and she struggled to hold back the tears.

"L'ho cresciuta, 'sa criatura"—"I raised her, this little creature," she would say when the subject of her leaving Tivoli came up.

"*A Madonna vi guardasse, tutt' i due*"—"May the Virgin Mary watch over you both."

Nonnie, Isabel, and I left Rhode Island for one last commute to Bard as an impromptu family. The violinist was waiting for us in Tivoli. When I pulled into the driveway with Nonnie and my daughter in tow, she was standing on the front porch with a chocolate bunny for Isabel. She approached Isabel like no other woman I had been with since Katherine's death. The others had cooed or gushed with well-intentioned goodwill, or they had played it cool, letting me know that they weren't about to become a Calabrian village of care in American translation. The violinist was exactly what Isabel needed from someone meeting her for the first time: relaxed and friendly, entirely natural.

And so on April 24, 2011, the seven-hundred-and-eleventh anniversary of Dante's journey to the Underworld on Easter in the year 1300, I made the most momentous introduction of my life:

"Helena, please meet Isabel."

KIDS CAN SENSE THE REAL thing from a mile away. Against all expectations, Isabel smiled when Helena said hello and quietly toddled alongside her as we went on our first walk together.

After spinning so many false pictures of makeshift families in my mind—whether walking on the beaches of Watch

Hill with Siena, or pushing strollers side by side with Astrid in Cobble Hill as if we were a couple with twins—I dared not dwell on this latest image of family harmony. It was way too soon to know whether the three of us would make it, but the possibility this time felt real. Helena asked me about our time in Rhode Island.

"A nightmare," I said.

"What did you expect?" she asked smiling.

"They're worried that Isabel is going to starve in protest over all the whole grains I'll try to feed her, and that I'll send her to school in clothes that don't match," I continued.

"Who can blame them?" she replied, still smiling.

My single parenthood would accelerate things between Helena and me, forcing us to confront the kinds of issues—Isabel's moods and needs, my family's place in her life—that most couples only arrive at after years together. But Helena would take it all in stride, and now we were walking the same ground I had covered in the snowy aftermath of Katherine's death, when not even the life of my new baby could rouse me from my conversations with the dead. *If the kernel of wheat dies*, Christ had spoken on Good Friday, *then it bears much fruit*. Dante had taken his journey to the Under-world on the same day Christ died, implying that his life too would be resurrected by Easter time when his trip through the dark wood ended days later. For one thousand and one days of grief and mourning I had watched my former life follow Katherine into the ground, wondering if it would ever bear the fruit that was now trying to push its way out of its buried kernel.

A MONTH LATER, and after four years of mothering her grand-daughter, Yolanda Luzzi left Tivoli. My brother, Angelo, came to New York from Rhode Island to pick her up—my mother had never learned to drive—while Isabel, Helena, and I prepared for a weekend away at her mentor's farm in upstate New York. The real good-bye had been a few weeks back during Easter; so my mom simply kissed Isabel and me as she left the house, and then gave us one of her *statti accortu* ("watch yourself") Calabrian benedictions, before gathering her things and climbing into the passenger seat of my broth-er's car.

My mom's final season with Isabel and me had been tense. As I took increased control of raising Isabel, I was invading what had been her turf with my obsessions over Isabel's healthy diet, my ban on TV, and my reading her nighttime stories. My mother could also feel Helena's growing importance in our lives, as she moved into a space that Yolanda had dutifully and lovingly occupied up to now. Even though she desired this change for Isabel and for me, it unsettled her.

One evening Helena and I asked Isabel to sit down for dinner with us, part of the new rule that banned eating in the living room. We even made her ultimate comfort food to take the edge off our new regime: a hot dog with macaroni and cheese.

Isabel would have none of it. My mom sat watching TV in the living room, brimming with suppressed disapproval but with her face as expressionless as it had been when she sat beside my father the day he had come to pull me off the tennis courts before the entire team. Meanwhile, Isabel shook the table with her cries and pounding. We held firm, but Isabel would not lose this battle. Breaking free of her high chair, she began to urinate on the kitchen floor in protest. My mother's enforced composure broke, and she stormed into the room.

"Ma che state facinna?" she shouted at me. *"A volite punira 'sa criatura?"*—"What are you doing? You want to punish this little creature?"

I was no stranger to being humiliated by my family—especially by my father, who had reserved his most ferocious tongue-lashings for me. Whenever I worked for him in our family garden, picking up debris or digging holes, he would shout one insult after another about my admittedly shoddy work, hurling at me such Calabrian curses as *"ti vo' sciupar' la faccia 'nu canu"*—"may a dog rip your face off." But it was nothing compared to the verbal castration administered by my mom in front of Helena: she had taken me down a peg in front of the woman I loved, suggesting that a real man—and a real father—would have mastered this debacle.

Isabel was sobbing; my mother stormed off to her room in the basement; Helena started crying and pushed me away when I tried to calm her. The relentless barrage of noise and acrimony had finally taken its toll on her. I stood alone in a puddle of urine in the kitchen while Isabel screamed for her Nonnie. The truth was, I had never learned to say no to Isabel. Having abdicated so much of her care to my mother and sisters, I was indulgent and smothering when we were together. I tried to win her favor with ice cream cones and stuffed animals, and lived in fear of her angry tears. To compensate for not spending enough time with her, I bent rules that should have been fixed when Isabel started to cry. Once, behind Helena's back, I replaced half of the vegetables that had provoked Isabel's outraged tears with familiar dollops of gooey orange mac and cheese.

"What are you doing?" Helena asked wide-eyed.

"Let's try to win this one with honey instead of vinegar," I said goofily, as Isabel inhaled the processed dairy and starch while pushing aside greens and sprouts.

"You're such a *Luzzi*," Helena scoffed, pronouncing the *z* with mocking softness, before storming out of the room.

The fallout from Nonnie's impending departure was straining my new relationship with Helena. We were walking a tightrope, and I didn't know if we would make it across. On more than one occasion, I accidentally called her Katherine without thinking—the name that I had locked inside me after the accident, the name that was too painful to utter, now came pouring out of my subconscious.

My last blowup with my mom had been over a cream-filled donut that I denied Isabel.

"*Non sapivo prima che tu fussi capace di chiste cose!*" she screamed at me—"I didn't know before that you were capable of stuff like this!" before adding, "*'Sa povera criatura . . . purtroppo 'n ci sto io a la guardare!*"—"This poor little creature . . . unfortunately I won't be here to watch over her!"

I could not help my mother deal with her emotions over this change in her life, the breakup of our family unit, and I wasn't angered over her outburst. Our Calabrian tribe of three was splitting up after four sad years together, during which she had raised Isabel and given me the space I needed to rebuild my life. I struggled to express my gratitude for what she did for me and Isabel, and that morning of her departure from Tivoli we were both too exhausted for loving, cathartic words. They would have to come later; that morning there was only relief, for her and for me.

Helena, Isabel, and I filled up my car for the trip north. The trunk and backseat groaned from the weight of Isabel's clothes and toys, a cooler of food, our luggage, and Helena's instruments. At one point, I had to jury-rig a contraption of clothes, belts, and bags to create a protective cushion for Helena's violin case. As I went to jam in the blue case, Helena sprang toward me.

"Please be careful," she said, her hand on my arm.

I didn't know it at the time, but her instrument was special. Very special.

A few days earlier, I had watched Helena play it during her production of *Bach Among Us*, a setting of Bach's music to dance. "The *Goldberg Variations*," she told the assembled crowd, "were commissioned by an insomniac Russian count."

The audience in Bard's cavernous Fisher Hall sat onstage in chairs surrounding the performers. Helena settled into her seat and began to play. She was wearing a flowing skirt and a halter, her hair in braids. The vision brought to mind Dante's Matelda, the gorgeous young maiden who appeared atop Mount Purgatory *cantando e scegliendo fior da fiore*, singing and gathering flower upon flower. Then the music started. The notes were rounded, almost buttery. Bach thought little of the variations, structured as they were around the endless repetition of a single harmonic structure. As she unraveled the braided notes Helena's beauty seemed otherworldly, fused as it was with luminous sound—delivered, no less, on a Stradivarius. The same instrument in the blue case that I would try to wedge between a bag of tennis rackets and cooler full of Go-Gurts for our trip upstate.

The instrument had been on a much more dramatic journey. In 1953 Sascha Jacobsen, concertmaster of the Los Angeles Philharmonic and steward of the violin, the so-called Red Diamond, was forced to abandon his car in a torrential downpour that almost cost him his life. The violin floated onto a beach near a golf course, and was found by a couple taking a walk. They took it to one of the world's great restorers, Hans Weisshaar, who worked for a year, using a specially designed tank to desalinate the instrument.

It is said that when Jacobsen got the instrument back, it sounded even better than before.

A violin reborn, the warped maple from Cremona drained of its salt by a skilled hand; Dante's voice as a poet restored by Beatrice's love, dissipating the bitter taste of exile's salty bread; and I, no longer locked in mute conversation with the dead, but immersed in the noisy joys of love and fatherhood.

THE TRANSITION TO LIFE WITHOUT Nonnie was not a smooth one. Helena's home was two streets away from us—she called it her escape hatch—but she was spending most of her time adjusting to life in her new Calabrian village. As much as Isabel enjoyed Helena's gift of the chocolate bunny and that first walk we all took together through Tivoli, she was not happy about the transfer of power away from her beloved grandma. When Helena showed up in our *nonna*-free environment, Isabel would greet her by stomping her feet and pointing to the door, and, with all the force that her thirty pounds could muster, she would shout, "Go home!" To make matters worse, Helena and I were suffering through sleepless nights, as Isabel would scream into the small hours, her bed just a few feet from ours in a makeshift bedroom separated by a sliding vinyl partition.

Helena had found her way into a house as sparse and empty as a barracks: there were no pictures on the walls, no newspapers or magazines to be found, only generic taupe furniture and stacks of scholarly books covered with Isabel's toys. I had been so imprisoned by my inward life of grief and mourning that I barely noticed the outside world. Within a month, Helena had ordered us a subscription to the *New York Times*, mounted some

paintings, and filled the walls with photos of our loved ones—
including the only photo of Katherine and me I could bear to
look at: the one of us holding each other in Greve in Chianti
is the proper name of the town, a town outside of Florence we
had visited a year before our marriage.

When Nonnie left Tivoli, Isabel's confusion over all the new
rules turned to bewilderment over a world in which the woman
she loved most of all could just suddenly disappear. She had
been told of her birth mother, Katherine, so it must have seemed
to her that she lived in a world where mothers come and go, and
fathers bring home nice ladies bearing gifts and promises of
ice cream. Only this time, the woman didn't always seem as
nice as the other ones, and she stuck around a lot longer. *Sure,*
Isabel's mind must have reasoned, *she pays a lot of attention to me,*
and she hugs and kisses me as Daddy does—but why can't I eat my hot
dog in front of Dora the Explorer *anymore?*

Helena and I had been together for just four months, and yet
she had already sloshed urine, thrown out soiled underwear,
and wiped away pools of tears—from Isabel's face and her own.

"Honey, I don't think I'm cut out for this," she told me after
one of Isabel's nuclear blowouts, as if anyone in the world was
cut out for walking into a wall of epic toddler resistance and
its ties to old Calabria. The ancient maternal protocols of my
family's culture did battle against Helena's progressive, organic, and no-nonsense approach to child rearing. Isabel had
been trained to reject everything that Helena had to offer, even
when it was the best thing in the world for her, for us. I had no

words of wisdom to offer Helena during this storm. I begged her to be patient. Clutching at straws, I tried to put Isabel's resistance in philosophical terms.

"Plato said that the philosopher king has to be high-spirited," I told her. "It's a prerequisite for greatness."

"Yeah," she answered. "Plato obviously never had to raise a raging brat."

But she was falling in love with this brat.

One evening that summer, Isabel kept soiling herself and acting out while we tried to sit down for dinner, and we put her in her room for a time-out. The manuals say that you are supposed to block your ears and keep the child safe and just go about your business until the child calms down, but the manuals had no chapter on my black swan of a daughter. The house shook from the hammering her three-year-old fists were giving to the bedroom door, and the wailing was pitched to stir the dead. By now, Helena and I were both in tears, and I could take it no more. I opened the door to find Isabel's mouth covered in blood.

She had bit her lip while screaming and was shaking with rage, beside herself over a new domestic arrangement that she did not, could not, would not accept. But Helena did not give up, nor did she storm out this time. She held Isabel, and I watched as she soothed my child. A miracle was taking place before my eyes, one as great as the split-second medical wonder that had kept Isabel among the living while Katherine slipped over to the other side. This second miracle was more attenuated and complicated, because there was no biology or science or instinct involved. It was a properly human miracle, born from a growing love between two strangers, a musician from St. Albans, England, and a young child from two villages, one in the Hudson Valley, and the other in the proverbial Calabrian village of my mother's care. Helena wiped the blood from Isabel's mouth and dried her tears, and they sat together on the tiny bed, surrounded by pictures. There was a photo of Nonnie holding Isabel during the long melancholic years when I struggled to rebuild my life; there was the Tuscan picture of Katherine and me, her raspberry lips mirroring our daughter's, the two of us bathed in sunshine in the middle of our brief season together. And now there was a new photo, one of Helena at age four, just about the same age as Isabel, sawing away on a miniature violin that was covered in her blond curls.

We were making it through, all of us—Isabel, Helena, and I—surviving a preposterous death and its fallout, and it was all because of a mother's love. The love of a Calabrian grandmother for her son and granddaughter, the love of an English violinist for a widower and his child. The food sat uneaten on the kitchen table. The child had no words to describe what tormented her. The man and the woman stood cluelessly in the room, still figuring out where their story was heading. It was all a messy work-in-progress, from the urine on the floor to the blood on the lip and the gallery of images on the wall. But in spite of the mess and the strife, there was a powerful force in the bedroom, like the wind that had whipped through Clermont on an early spring day, when the yellow and green leaves filled the air, shedding a blessing upon us as they fell to the earth, just as the dying seed of grain gives birth to a field of wheat.

THE TREES OF THE BERKSHIRES continued to sway as Helena descended the bottomless ladder of the four-bar bass line, its variations as expansive as the love Bach apparently felt for his deceased wife, Maria. By now, Isabel was worn out from her wrangling and had settled into a stupor on my lap. She was exhausted, hungry—maybe even a bit spellbound by the music.

As the piece wound to its conclusion, I heard a clue in the music, the key I'd been looking for all these years after Katherine's death. It wasn't a sense of joy after sorrow that I heard in the chaconne; that would be obvious enough and, in the manner of every time-heals-all-wounds narrative, dishonest—something worn away by attrition rather than healed. It was the music's joy *within* the sorrow that arrested me. It was irrational. Erotic. Passionate. Everything that deep and true love is. Everything that deep and true love remains, even after the person who inspires that love is no longer.

The task of writing *Paradiso* was formidable for Dante because in heaven every story that he once knew took on a new form— what seemed like true love, Francesca's for Paolo, turned out to be lust; what seemed like a curse, Dante's exile from Florence, turned out to be a blessing. Every love story is potentially a grief story, Julian Barnes once wrote. But by the time Dante got to *Paradiso* he understood it was actually the other way around.

Bach's descending four-bar bass line may have been a continuous expression of grief, but that was only part of the story. It was also a declaration of love, which is as open-ended and filled with mystery as death is unyielding and empty. Helena coaxed the strings to the summit of the chaconne, which ended where it started: in the bittersweet union of love and loss, in the bearing of witness to the love for another person who is no more. Listening to the music, I realized that I had misunderstood Katherine's death, for the simple and inescapable reason that I had been staring at it for years through filters of grief. I had been looking at it with one eye only—only love could give me back full vision.

That's it, I thought, watching the blur of Helena's fingers, feeling Isabel's body against my own, *every grief story is a love story.*

Epilogue

In June 2012, a year after Helena and I had lain there together on a leaf-filled blanket—and a year before she would coax the joy and sorrow from Bach's chaconne—she and I returned to Clermont. The leaden gray sky where I had fallen in love with this English woman from St. Albans was now deep blue, and the snappy wind of that raw spring day had given way to breezeless sunshine. I was back along the Hudson with Helena, and this time we weren't alone. Isabel was there with us, with flowers in her hair. Nonnie had come along as well, and even put on a dress for the occasion. The chaplain who had spoken about motherhood five years earlier in Bard's Chapel of the Innocents at

Katherine's memorial service was also there, and this time he had an infinitely easier task. At least it was supposed to be. But he had taken the wrong Bible for the ceremony, mistakenly bringing the Hebrew original instead of the English translation, and so he had to sight-translate as all looked on in the Cutting Garden.

Helena's dad was there, as were her brother and the sister who looked nothing like her yet was undoubtedly her twin, the taut bond stretching like invisible wire between them. As the chaplain spoke and the guests settled into their white foldout seats in the garden, Helena's father played a Bach prelude, the undulating, meditative quality of the piece filled the warm air as even the children stood still to listen. It was all repetitions with slight variations, just like the mournful love letter of the chaconne. Helena's sister stood beside her, and her mother and brother watched from the crowd, the first time in years that her dispersed family all gathered in one place.

Isabel wanted nothing to do with me that day, for she was too beguiled by the dresses and the flowers and the games she was playing with the other children. When she wasn't running around, she stayed close to Helena's side, the woman she called Mom and Mama, sometimes even an exaggerated May-May when she wanted something. As soon as the ceremony ended, Isabel burst out into the green expanses, part of a fluffy white train of other children relieved that the music had stopped, the rings had been exchanged, and a kiss had sealed the affair.

Just a year earlier, Isabel had screamed in bloody protest when the only mother she had ever known, her *nonna*, was being replaced by someone unfamiliar to her in every way. Now a vibrant and hyperarticulate four, Isabel bore little resemblance to the little girl who clung to Nonnie's skirts like a lemur. Part of it was developmental, the normal course of growth, but part of it was the new love that had knocked me out of my one-thousand-and-one-day torpor and driven from our home its cloud of grief and sorrow. Yolanda had no more harsh words for me by now; all the bitterness of our final days as a makeshift family had dissipated.

"*Volevo parlare anch'io*"—"I too wanted to talk"—she said as she cradled my face in her hands, after all the others at the long reception tables had made their speeches.

"*Cosa volevi dire, mamma?*" I asked—"What did you want to say?"

"I don't know—I just wanted to speak."

With her broken English and fragmented Calabrian, my mother was not about to stand up and deliver an oration. But had she spoken, she could have described her decision, that day Katherine died, to become a mother again and help me raise Isabel. She might have told of how she knew that she had to give up the freedom that had finally come to her in old age to return to the stench of soiled diapers, the touchy moods of a grieving husband, and her home confinement in a college town far from her family. My mother said none of these things because she was not one to sing her own praises. Her life had been for others, and that was how it would remain: with her at the center of a loving constellation that made speeches unnecessary.

There were many groups on the lawns and under the tent: the Bard crowd flecked in gray, a bow tie or two, in floral prints and pastel dresses; my friends, still *sportlich* and spry in their forties, reminding me at every turn of my dumb luck, asking Helena with a laugh if she knew what she was getting into, while she smiled saying it's too late to back out now; Katherine's family, heroically imposing none of their sadness, eating and drinking and dancing and speaking only of the future of our new family, and of Isabel's new mother. I stood in the midst of it all, a bit bewildered, as suddenly four years didn't seem like it had been so long after all.

And yet it had been. It had been monstrously long, as though a million years had separated the life that was before November 29, 2007, from the life that came after. If I had counted them all, these days and years in the Underworld of grief and mourning, the number would have made me shudder as I stood there in my gray suit and white tie. I looked down the Hudson and thought of the one hundred and sixty thousand acres that the British crown had given the first owners of Clermont, the Livingston family, and how I too had been given an outsized gift. They were a blur now, all the people hugging me, smiling into my eyes, and laughing into my ears, men in black jackets and women in red dresses, everyone light-headed from the Prosecco, the sunlight on the roses, the sight of galloping children on the green fields. She had said *I do*, this violinist, the woman who would shape the chords of the chaconne in the Berkshires and inspire me to write this story. She was the only one who could do it, because she alone had gently lifted the sad story festering inside me and replaced it with another one. More than this, she had been the one to insist that I write down the stories that I had been telling only to myself in silence. She had begun to read my work just as she had begun to love me and then my child. Her eyes had been the first to see the tales I told myself on those commutes between Tivoli and Westerly transformed into rough drafts. She did more than dare me to live a life of meaning—she asked me to put it into words.

KATHERINE'S DEATH WOULD BRING WITH it boundless chaos and flux, but there was one constant throughout the entire aftermath. My reading of Dante had always been deep and personal, but when I found myself in the dark wood, his words became a matter of life and death. He had taught me that you can love somebody without a body in a certain way, but that you must reserve your truest love for somebody whose breath you can hear and feel—your child's, your wife's—and that you may visit the Underworld but you cannot live there. He also taught that self-pity is no substitute for free will, just as the electric air of grief is not the kind that can sustain your breathing in real life.

Is there a part of us that outlives the body? The question tormented me after Katherine's death, making me agonize for the first time over whether we have a soul. It brought me back to the book and the author I loved above all others. "*Consider the meaning that is hidden / beneath the veil of these strange verses,*" Dante once wrote, and I began to discover new layers of meaning in his poem that I had never approached as a scholar. Not even Dante, a deeply Christian writer who ends his poem face-to-face with God, could know for certain whether we have a soul. But his *Divine Comedy* was born from the belief that literature can transform you through *lungo studio e grande amore*, and in surrendering to beautiful writing we begin what an astute reader of Dante, the poet Keats, called soul-making: how we must face "a World of Pains and troubles" in order to realize our true selves and our full humanity.

I had always wondered how, after all those bitter years of wandering, Dante could end his poem with a message of peace, but there on the banks of Clermont I had my answer. I now understood that every grief story is indeed a love story—it was love that had landed me in the dark wood to begin with, and only love could lead me out. As Beatrice had taught Dante, you can't have love without faith and hope and joy. Helena's love had rescued us. And now my love for Helena was bringing me full circle to some of the earliest words that Dante ever wrote:

Incipit vita nova
Here begins the new life

Dearest Isabel, you know by now that I can't retrace those first steps of ours any more than a writer can take back his first words. Your life began in the glare of an emergency room, and our first days together found me staring at you through the bars of your crib, exiled from the fatherhood I had always dreamed of, with no words to help me fathom our broken bond.

But I hope you'll discover, as I have, that it's not what lands you in the dark wood that defines you, but what you do to make it out—just as you can't understand the first words of a story until you've read the last ones.

Here begins the new life. When you read Dante, you'll see that these early words of his point all the way to his last ones, when he looked back on hell, purgatory, and heaven, just as I look back now on our time in the Underworld and our journey to Clermont. He had the courage to believe in love, no matter how much he suffered, how much horror he endured. And it's with love and all its mysteries—not God or justice or free will or hope—that Dante chooses to end his poem, a vision I hope with all my heart will one day be yours:

In a Dark Wood

Già volgeva il mio disio e 'l velle,
sì come rota ch'igualmente è mossa,
l'amor che move il sole e l'altre stelle.

Now my will and my desire were turned,
like a wheel in perfect motion,
by the Love that moves the sun and the other stars.

Translations and Notes

"Nothing joined by musical bonds can be taken from one language to another without destroying all its sweetness or harmony," Dante once wrote, and indeed, anybody who tries to translate Dante confronts this grim literary reality in an especially visceral way. His original meaning is so bound up with specific Tuscan words and turns of phrase, and the music of his poem so beholden to his precise meter and rhyming tercets, that carrying him over into a foreign language can make you feel like you're trying to square a circle. Yet there have been many heroic and valuable attempts to "English" Dante, beginning with the first full American translation, Longfellow's brilliant mix of scholarly

and poetic renderings in 1867, and including important sub-
sequent versions by John Sinclair (1939), Charles Singleton
(1970–6), Allen Mandelbaum (1980–4), and Robert and Jean
Hollander (2000–7). Recent translations by poets ranging from
Seamus Heaney and W. S. Merwin to Robert Pinsky and Clive
James, among many others, have also enriched Dante's afterlife
in the English language. I invite the reader to explore the rich
history of Dante in translation in whatever happens to be your
madrelingua, mother tongue—and I especially encourage you to
begin to study Italian so that you can read Dante in the original, where the magic truly happens.

The translations from Dante's *Divine Comedy* in this book
are my own. My practice has been to try to translate Dante
as close to the original as possible, following his poem line by
line. Since I'm no *poeta*, I did not attempt to render his verse
in English meter. My aim throughout has been for clarity and
transparency, hoping that, despite my inevitably impoverished
English refractions of Dante's Tuscan, the reader might glean
the sweetness and harmony of his original music.

I have also followed this practice in my translations from
Dante's *primo amico*, Guido Cavalcanti. References to Homer's
Odyssey are to Richard Lattimore's landmark version and Ian
McKellen's moving narration of the translation by Robert
Fagles (New York: Penguin, 1996) in the audiobook from 1999.
Translations from foreign sources are my own, unless indicated
otherwise below in this list of works cited in my book:

Julian Barnes, *Levels of Life*, New York: Knopf, 2013.

Teodolinda Barolini, "'Only Historicize': History, Material Culture (Food, Clothes, Books), and the Future of Dante Studies," in *Dante Studies* 127 (2009).

Umberto Bosco, ed., *Enciclopedia dantesca*, Rome: Istituto della Enciclopedia Italiana, 1970-8.

Byron, *The Works of Lord Byron*, ed. Ernest Hartley Coleridge, London: Murray, 1905.

Guido Cavalcanti, *The Poetry of Guido Cavalcanti*, ed. Lowry Nelson, 1968.

Carlo Collodi, *Le avventure di Pinocchio*, Milan: Mondadori, 1981.

Dante, *La Commedia secondo l'antica vulgata*, ed. Giorgio Petrocchi, Milan: Mondadori, 1966-8.

———. *Vita Nuova*, ed. Domenico De Robertis, Milan-Naples: Ricciardi, 1984. English translation, *Dante's Vita Nuova*, trans. Mark Musa, Bloomington: Indiana University Press, 1973.

T.S. Eliot, *Prufrock and Other Observations*, 1920.

———. *Selected Prose of T. S. Eliot*, ed. Frank Kermode, New York: Harcourt, Brace, Jovanovich, 1975.

Homer, *Odyssey*, trans. Richard Lattimore, New York: Harper and Row, 1965.

Victor Hugo, *Complete Works*, ed. Pierre Martino, Paris: Ollendorff, 1925.

James Joyce, *Dubliners*, London: Penguin, 1993.

John Keats, *Selected Letters*, ed. Jon Mee, Oxford: Oxford University Press, 2009.

Rudyard Kipling, *Collected Poems of Rudyard Kipling*, London: Wordsworth Editions, 1994.

Giuseppe Mazzotta, "Life of Dante," in *The Cambridge Companion to Dante*, ed. Rachel Jacoff, Cambridge: Cambridge University Press, 1993.

Ivan Turgenev, *Fathers and Sons*, trans. Richard Freeborn, Oxford: Oxford University Press, 2008.

Virgil, *Aeneid*, trans. Robert Fagles, New York: Penguin, 2006.

Acknowledgments

Nobody understands our need for the right kind of guidance better than Dante, who turned first to Virgil and then to Beatrice to navigate his way out of the *selva oscura*, the dark wood. I too have been blessed by the support and advice of those closest to me. My agent and friend, Joy Harris, has nurtured this project from its earliest and most uncertain stages. With the deepest caring and insight, she has helped my book find its voice. Once *In a Dark Wood* began to take shape, I had the great fortune to begin working with Karen Rinaldi, the editor whose brilliance and instincts for emotional depth infuse every page. Karen had the belief and courage to ask me to dig deep, pushing me beyond my natural reserve into uncharted, sometimes uncomfortable territory. It was this dialogue between her editing and my writing that enabled me to fathom the true depths of Dante's message. Dantesque souls to the core, Karen and Joy have shown me how the spirit of *The Divine Comedy* can infuse our everyday lives.

The manuscript's journey from a brief op-ed piece in the *New York Times* to the published edition before you has been a long and circuitous one, aided at every turn by my beloved wife, Helena Baillie, whose sharp editorial eye and extraordinary artistic feel rescued the book at crucial moments. My dear friends and trusted readers, Scott McGill and Ross Guberman, offered invaluable insights at key junctures, forcing me to leave my scholarly comfort zone and think about why Dante matters to us today. I have benefited from the extraordinary efforts of my entire team at HarperCollins, especially those I have had the privilege of working with most closely: Jane Beirn, Penny Makras, and Hannah Robinson.

My greatest debt of gratitude is nonliterary. My mother, Yolanda Luzzi, and my siblings, Angelo, Margaret, Mary, Rose, and Tina, took Isabel and me in at a time when my own instincts for survival and caring for another person had been severely compromised by Katherine's sudden death. With sustained and selfless love, they nurtured my daughter and healed my own broken spirit, never asking for anything in return, and always seeking to restore what death had stolen. Dante ends his poem by admitting that there is no way to describe the majesty and mystery of creation, when he is granted a glimpse of God's handiwork at the summit of Paradiso. Sometimes words just fail. Humbled by the scope of my family's generosity, I can only say in their language and Dante's, *grazie di cuore*.

For years, my wish to write this book was haunted by the image of a family that almost never was: my daughter, Isabel, and I, as our first years together transpired in the midst of a grief that blinded me to the joys and responsibilities of fatherhood. The gift of Helena's arrival into our life, along with Dante's wisdom, helped change all this, and restore a father-daughter bond that death had shattered. I dedicate this book to Isabel because, more than anything, it was my love for her that saved me from the dark wood.

Our *piccola famiglia* was blessed with a new arrival just as I was putting the finishing touches on *In a Dark Wood*: the birth of our son, James Baillie Luzzi. And it is for James and Isabel that I write these final words, among the first that Dante ever wrote, and the ones that sum up everything they mean to me:

Incipit vita nova

Here begins the new life.

About the Author

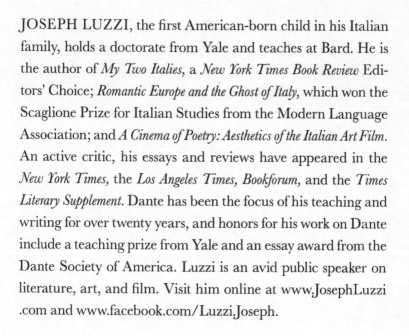

JOSEPH LUZZI, the first American-born child in his Italian family, holds a doctorate from Yale and teaches at Bard. He is the author of *My Two Italies*, a *New York Times Book Review* Editors' Choice; *Romantic Europe and the Ghost of Italy*, which won the Scaglione Prize for Italian Studies from the Modern Language Association; and *A Cinema of Poetry: Aesthetics of the Italian Art Film*. An active critic, his essays and reviews have appeared in the *New York Times*, the *Los Angeles Times, Bookforum*, and the *Times Literary Supplement*. Dante has been the focus of his teaching and writing for over twenty years, and honors for his work on Dante include a teaching prize from Yale and an essay award from the Dante Society of America. Luzzi is an avid public speaker on literature, art, and film. Visit him online at www.JosephLuzzi .com and www.facebook.com/Luzzi.Joseph.